EQUIP
Series

Deacons
Clarifying the Biblical Role

J. Robert Douglas

With All Wisdom Publications
Cupertino, CA

Deacons
Clarifying the Biblical Role

Deacons: Clarifying the Biblical Role
Copyright © 2022 J. Robert Douglas
Published by WITH ALL WISDOM PUBLICATIONS

Requests for information about WITH ALL WISDOM PUBLICATIONS can be sent to:

editor@withallwisdom.org

All rights reserved.

ISBN: 978-1-952221-08-8

Scripture quotations are from the ESV® Bible (The Holy Bible, English Standard Version®), copyright © 2001 by Crossway, a publishing ministry of Good News Publishers. Used by permission. All rights reserved.

Scripture quotations taken from the (NASB®) New American Standard Bible®, Copyright © 1960, 1971, 1977, 1995, 2020 by The Lockman Foundation. Used by permission. All rights reserved. www.lockman.org

---

Editor-in-Chief: Cliff McManis
General Editor: Derek Brown
Managing Editor: Breanna Paniagua
Cover Design: J. Robert Douglas
Proofreaders: Tim Anderson, Albert Chen, Gary Leith, John Platz

This work is a publication of WITH ALL WISDOM PUBLICATIONS. No part of this publication may be reproduced, stored in a retrieval system, or transmitted in any form or by any means except by permission of the publisher.

To my father, Mel Douglas, a mentor and a tremendous model for serving in Christ's church whom the Lord has used in numerous capacities, including being both an elder and a deacon.

To my pastor, Cliff McManis, a close friend, a mentor, and a true brother alongside whom I am blessed to serve and who encouraged me to write this book.

To the past and present faithful deacons of Creekside Bible Church: Adam Albright, Robert Anderson, Kyle Asire, Aaron Holsteen, James Hong, Ken Medeiros, Jason Ng, Nathan Ng, Stephen Salinas, Darren Terry, and David Tong—all great men of God alongside whom I have been privileged to work for a number of years. These men are a tremendous blessing to me, the Creekside elders, and the church body.

Acknowledgements

Thank you to my wife, Robin—an amazing woman of God who has loved and supported me throughout our marriage. God has led us on an amazing journey for thirty-two years with some daunting twists and turns. I am looking forward to what God still has for us and walking though it together.

A special thank you to the With All Wisdom editors, without whom I could not have finished this book. Cliff McManis, Derek Brown, and Breanna Paniagua put in tremendous time and effort. Their grace-filled insights, hard work, and encouragement are a blessing to me and are what helped make this book possible.

Contents

	Foreword	i
	Frequently Asked Questions	1
	Introduction	5
1	Christ, the Head of the Church	9
2	From Simplicity to Bureaucracy	13
3	The Meaning of "Deacon"	27
4	From Acts 6 to 1 Timothy 3	37
5	The Selection Process and Qualifications	63
6	The Ministry of a Deacon	97
7	Christ's Promise to Deacons	111
8	Who are the Women in 1 Timothy 3:11?	115
9	Conclusion	141
	Appendix 1 – Best Practices	149
	Appendix 2 – Raising Up Deacons	181
	Bibliography	cxcvii
	Scripture Index	cxcvii

Foreword

"As the leadership goes, so go the people." That's an old adage that has proven itself true over the years, generation after generation. A group of people, and organization, is only as strong as its leadership. And rarely do people rise above their leadership. Nowhere is that more true than in the local church. When it comes to spiritual health, many times for the individual, that health is in large measure impacted by the health of the church leadership. Leadership matters.

Sadly, in this day and age, many Christians don't consider the importance of leadership in the local church and the impact it can have, positively or adversely, on the people in that church. Some argue that the Bible gives no details of any particular leadership structure for the church. But Jesus put a premium on quality leadership, and its importance, in the local church. This is why Jesus invested more time in His few apostles for three-plus years than He invested in anyone else. He knew they would become the first leadership team of the church. The twelve apostles would lay the foundation of the church and serve as the first pastors of the church in Jerusalem.

Paul also put a premium on training quality church leaders. He believed leadership mattered. He gave to the church perpetual leadership qualifications in 1 Timothy 3 and Titus 1 to guarantee each local church was led by spiritual leaders who loved God, had integrity and were gifted at leading. And in those two passages he delineated the two formal leadership offices of the church: elders and deacons. And since then God has expected every local church to implement God's leadership structure He has laid out, starting with the two biblical offices of elder and deacon.

In this book, Pastor Douglas accentuates in detail God's priorities for local church leadership by giving an excellent exposition of what a biblical deacon is. The role of deacon has been egregiously misunderstood and compromised all throughout church history, beginning a short time after the apostles died. Through the years some have confused the role of deacon with that of pastor or overseer, expanding the role beyond what God intended. Some minimize the office of deacon, consigning the deacons of the church to the sideline with no authority while bogging them down with trivial duties the pastor (or others) refuses to undertake. Some have neglected the office of deacon altogether, virtually ignoring that it is in Scripture, as they try to run their churches with man-made wisdom and man-made counterfeit models.

With more than twenty-five years of church leadership experience, and as one who currently serves as an elder who works directly with the team of deacons at our church, Pastor Douglas writes with a passion for the sacred office of deacon while giving a thoroughly biblical overview of the role in a practical manner. This book is ideal for any local church pastor or elder who wants to make sure his use of deacons is in sync with the plum-line of Scripture. It is also ideal for training prospective deacons in your local church. Seminary students and church-planters will find it to be an invaluable resource as well to be reminded of the biblical priorities of the office that

Foreword

are often forgotten about in the shadows. The principles herein as outlined by Pastor Douglas are tried and true as we have been leaning on them in the training of our deacons since 2006. God has honored our pursuit to preserve the biblical model of deacon. I trust you will be refreshed and blessed by this good read as we have been.

Pastor Cliff McManis
Creekside Bible Church
Cupertino, CA
October, 2022

Frequently Asked Questions

In conversations with fellow believers, I have found that when the topic of church leadership is addressed, there are more questions about the position, role and service of a deacon than about anything else. Below are some of the most common questions I receive:

What is the difference between an elder and a deacon?
Elders are the spiritual leaders of the local church. Deacons are servant-leaders of the church. See chapters four and six.

Is it wrong for a church to have deaconesses?
It is not necessarily wrong but is it not the best practice. Women can hold many essential ministry leadership positions vital to a church. Scripture does not allow for women to hold formal church leadership positions of elder or deacon. If a church has women deacons or deaconesses it can cause confusion and possibly diminish the true office of deacons. See chapter eight.

Is there a difference between deaconesses and women deacons?
Proponents of women deacons believe there should be both male and female deacons and that there is no difference in their respective roles. Similarly, proponents of deaconesses see them as female helpers to male deacons or elders who are not part of church leadership. See chapter eight.

Aren't all who serve in the church really deacons?
No. There is a difference between those with a gift of service and those who have the gift and a calling to become a servant-leader. The office of deacon is a leadership position. Other saints may also have the gift of service. Deacons have to be

identified by the elders and affirmed by the congregation as qualified leaders according to 1 Timothy 3:8-12. See chapter six.

Are deacons actually elders in training?
No. Elders and deacons are two different positions with different qualifications and roles. This does not mean a man who is a deacon cannot become an elder. But the office of deacon is not a stepping-stone for the elder role. See chapters two and six.

Are deacons teachers?
All believers have at least one spiritual gift. All deacons have the gift of service (cf. Rom 12:7). Some deacons have additional gifts including the gift of teaching. All elders must be able to teach (1 Tim 3:2).

Should there be a "future" deacon training program?
It is good for elders to be regularly in the process recognizing potential future leaders and working with them to identify, develop and amplify their gifts. To suggest to a man the possibility of becoming a leader before first assessing his gifts and qualifications will impose an undue burden on him. This practice can lead to men becoming disgruntled, disillusioned, and even divisive. See the appendix on Raising up Deacons.

How many years should the length of term be for a deacon?
Scripture does not designate a term or duration for deacons to serve. Many in the church are proponents of designating a certain number of years and rotation, while others see it as a lifetime appointment. See chapter six and the appendix on Best Practices.

What is the purpose and rationale for term-specific appointments, and can those be defended as biblically-based versus being merely the residue of human wisdom?
My pastor taught me to always ask the question. "Where is it in the Bible?" Frequently man's thinking and corporate culture

have crept into church leadership models. As with anything in the Christian life, we need to make sure our view is biblically based and not steeped in tradition, culture, man's wisdom, or personal preferences. See chapter six.

How many deacons should a church have?
As many as the elders need. See chapters four and six.

How does a church choose a deacon?
Acts 6 and 1 Timothy 3 demonstrate processes initiated and overseen by apostles/elders that include examination by the entire church guided by the elders and end with ordination of the new deacon by elders. See chapter five and appendix on Best Practices.

Don't deacons just manage the church's money? Or just minister to the poor?
Deacons are to serve and manage wherever the elders direct. Some church elders have deacons to serve in a few select areas, while others direct deacons to serve across many ministries. In 1 Timothy 3 the apostle Paul gives elders autonomy to choose how and where deacons will serve. Scripture simply exhorts, "let the deacons serve." See chapter five.

Can a deacon become an elder?
Yes. Deacons have the spiritual gift of serving and qualifications in 1 Timothy 3:8-12. Elders are gifted in wisdom, leadership, serving, shepherding/teaching, and have different qualifications than deacons (1 Tim 3:1-7; Titus 1:5-9). So, a man who would go from deacon to elder must demonstrate the proper gifts and qualifications. See chapter six.

Are the seven men in Acts 6 deacons?
The formal office of deacon was not universalized until thirty years after the events described in Acts 6. Technically, the seven men of Acts 6 were not deacons. That said, the foundation for deacons was laid in Acts 6. By selecting and ordaining these seven men, the apostles initiated an office of

the church that would be universalized thirty years later by the Apostle Paul. See chapter four.

Should I attend a church where deacons serve in the elder role?
It is not wrong to attend a church with a non-biblical leadership structure. But don't be surprised when problems come. See chapter nine.

Introduction

I was blessed to be raised by strong Christian parents. They were wonderful models in their roles as husband and wife, as parents, and as believers involved in serving their church. Over the years I watched and learned leadership from my father who served as a deacon in several churches and also as an elder. At one point he served as the President of the Executive Board for the Southern Baptist Convention in California.

In sixty years of life, I have served in several churches across a variety of roles, ranging from basic service to the preaching and teaching of God's Word to the role of shepherding as an elder. In my current pastoral role, one of my duties is oversight of our deacons. This includes everything from coordination of their service activities to the ongoing teaching and training of these men as they serve Christ's Church.

For years I have been looking for a concise book to give our deacons that would provide a historical survey, a proper biblical view of deacons and their roles, and a written model of how deacons fit into the leadership structure of the local church. What I found—and what is nothing short of astonishing to me—is that such a book has been hard to find! This critical office, established by the Apostles through the direction of the Holy Spirit, has straightforward and clearly identifiable duties and responsibilities. However, through a combination of faulty exegesis of Scripture, smothering human tradition, and a barrage of personal preferences, the office of deacon has become a muddled mess across the landscape of the Christian church. Based on my personal experience, this should not come as much of a surprise. I have seen the confusion, first-hand, in the churches in which I served over the years. Through my personal experiences, I became familiar with the various divergent views and types of wrong thinking about the office and role of deacons.

This is not to say that all the books on deacons that I have read are bad. Most had very helpful information. However, I could not find, in a single source, a biblically based, comprehensive work that provided the practical essentials for the office of deacon—from its basic definition, origin, qualifications, use in the New Testament, to its implementation in today's local church.

In short, I found the landscape of views for the office of deacons to be vast, under-developed and conflicted with each other.

There is widespread disparity among churches on the purpose, role, position, and qualifications of a deacon. I even found leaders within the same denomination or those with the same theological perspective not always agreeing. I find this odd because church leadership structure is not a minor biblical issue. Variance between differing denominations and between differing theological systems is expected. However, it was surprising to me to see scholars, commentators, pastors and denominational leaders *who come from the same theological persuasion* disagree on something as foundational as the role of the second office of the church. Disparate views on church leadership roles are not novel and especially where, as regards the office of deacon, the wilderness of disagreement has existed for centuries. These competing views on the deacon role started within a few hundred years of when the church began in the first century. For 1,800-plus years the church has had splintering and competing views over this critical office. But the good news is that truth on this matter has not been completely lost nor abandoned.

Christ is the Head of the Church (Eph 5:23) and he said, "I will build My church" (Matt 16:18). Jesus gave clear and sufficient information about his Church's intended structure and function, including its leadership. Jesus sent the Holy Spirit and commissioned his apostles to establish two offices that were designed to work in harmony to serve his people. Jesus' expectations of the two church offices, elder and deacon, have been faithfully preserved in the written Word. With that truth in mind, this book will lean upon the established doctrines of biblical sufficiency, inerrancy, and perspicuity in pursuit of the Bible's clear teaching on the office of deacon. It is my hope that this book will provide a clear biblical view of the office of deacon, and that its scope will faithfully cover not only salient deacon-specific topics from history and theology, but also the daily practical elements of being a deacon.

The Scope of This Book

We will start by reviewing the commands of Christ regarding his Church, followed by a look at church history and the confusion created by men in church leadership. Next, I will give a word study of "deacon" (*diakonos*) in its proper context, followed by an analysis of how the office of deacon was initiated in Acts 6 and then universalized in 1 Timothy 3. Then will follow a study of the qualifications, the selection process, and the proper scope of a deacon's ministry. We will end by addressing the issue of women deacons, the promise of Christ for deacons and best practices for churches around the office of deacon.

Jesus said, "**I will build My church** and the gates of hell shall not prevail against it."
Matthew 16:18

The Apostle Paul said, "**Christ is the head of the church**, his body, and is himself its Savior."
Ephesians 5:23

1

Christ, the Head of the Church

A truth that is regularly missed or only nominally addressed by many authors of church leadership is the fact that Jesus Christ is the Head of the church. He is the Savior who gives believers eternal life and communion with God (1 Cor 15:1-4). Christ has power over heaven and earth, and complete authority over all believers and the church (Matt 7:21-23; 28:18). Christ is the Savior who freely gave himself for the church and is the unquestionable Head of the church (Eph 5:23, 25).

- He determined when the church began (Acts 2:1-47)
- He is the Chief Shepherd of the church (1 Pet 5:4)
- He chose the apostles and appointed them as the church's first leaders (John 21:17)
- He determined the church leadership structure (1 Tim 3:1-13)
- He grows his church at his pleasure (Matt 16:18)
- He sanctifies the church (Eph 5:26)
- He loves and nourishes his church (Eph 5:29).
- He intercedes for his church at the right hand of the Father (Rom 8:34)

- The church is to follow Christ's leadership (Eph 5:24)
- He will return for his church (John 14:2-3)

Christ has never abdicated, to finite man, his role as Head of the church. It is not man's position to "take the reins" and redesign any aspect of Christ's church, including the form and structure of its leadership. Few understood this better than the sixteenth century reformer, John Calvin. He considered the God-ordained leadership offices of the church as primary, not secondary, or tertiary or negotiable as many believe today. In his *Institutes*, clarifying the office of deacon, Calvin wrote on this subject, warning believers, "Now seeing that in the sacred assembly all things ought to be done decently and in order (1 Cor 14:40), there is nothing in which this ought to be more carefully observed than in settling government, irregularity in any respect being nowhere more perilous."[1] In other words, to mess with Christ's church leadership structure is dangerous. For instance, in today's contemporary evangelical church there is a growing trend to abolish the office of deacon. No local church or pastor is allowed to whimsically decide, "We don't need deacons."

Sadly, many churches have done just that. Christ is the Head of his church. He is the Chief Shepherd (1 Pet 5:4). He is the Bridegroom (Eph 5:25-27); He is divine (John 10:27-30). He is infinite and eternal (John 1:1-5; Isa 40:6-31). Man is finite and fallen (Ps 90). Christ gave specific instructions to the apostles on the structure of church leadership. Today it is the job of elders and deacons to properly understand the truth of God's Word and follow the leadership of Christ as under-shepherds

---

[1] John Calvin, *Institutes of the Christian Religion*, translated by Henry Beveridge (Peabody, MA: Hendrickson Publishers, 2008), IV.3.10.

and servants of his bride, the church. Elders and deacons are servants of Christ. They tend to the flock of Christ's sheep (John 21:17) and will give an account to God the judge for their service (Heb 13:17). Neither the church or its leaders have the authority to change any element of the position or purpose of an elder or deacon. Christ rules by the Word of God. Scripture was his defense when tempted by Satan (Matt 4:1-11). Scripture was his weapon when addressing false teachers (Matt 12:1-8). And in the Sermon on the Mount, Christ tells us that all will not be completed until every single letter, and every little jot of God's Word is accomplished (Matt 5:18). It is abundantly clear that Christ requires the precise application of Scripture.

The precision in which we handle God's Word, therefore, is enormously important. The last command of the New Testament is witness to this responsibility:

> I warn everyone who hears the words of the prophecy of this book: if anyone adds to them, God will add to him the plagues described in this book, and if anyone takes away from the words of the book of this prophecy, God will take away his share in the tree of life and in the holy city, which are described in this book (Rev 22:18-19).

This book is about church leadership and, specifically, the position and role of deacons. Our study will be focused from God's Word and Christ's instructions for his deacons, as opposed to human tradition, denominational precedents, or contemporary pragmatic business strategies. We will look at how Christ initiated the office of deacon, how he universalized the office and what he expects from the ministry of his deacons.

"For those who guide this people are leading them astray; And those who are guided by them **are brought to confusion**."
Isaiah 9:16

2

From Simplicity to Bureaucracy

Although the apostle Paul through the direction of the Holy Spirit universalized church leadership with a simple two-office structure—elders and deacons—this New Testament biblical model was compromised not long into the post-apostolic church. A new, man-made office of "regional bishop" was introduced, creating a three-tiered hierarchical leadership structure. The regional bishop oversaw multiple local churches and their respective elders and deacons.[1] This became burdensome for deacons, who now had to serve in functional duties assigned by *both* the bishop and the elders.[2] As time went on, churches became even more hierarchical by adding more

---

[1] "Early in the second century, monoepiscopacy (a singular bishop ruling over a local church) was being encouraged by church leaders such as Ignatius, and at this time the threefold ministry of bishop, presbyter, and deacon became well established. Around 100-115AD, faced with a dangerous heresy and confronted with potential divisions in churches, Ignatius responded with a new form of church government. He made a distinction between the offices of bishop and the presbyter/elder and called for 'one bishop, together with the presbytery and the deacons,' to lead the churches. In one sense, both the bishop and the elders exercised authority over the church. However, Ignatius also elevated the office of bishop over that of elder; the position of deacon was under both of these offices...Thus, a three-tiered hierarchy was erected, with the bishop exercising ultimate authority. Accordingly, unity with and obedience to the bishop was indispensable." Gregg R. Allison, *Sojourners and Strangers: The Doctrine of the Church* (Wheaton, IL: Crossway, 2012), 257. "Bishop" is a biblical word and is synonymous with "elder," but its meaning was distorted, expanded, and misused right after the apostles died.

[2] J.D. O'Donnell, *Handbook for Deacons* (Nashville, TN: Randall House Publications, 1973), 13-14.

layers of professional clergy who then dominated all elements of leadership, operations, and finances.

By the fourth century, the Christian faith became the official religion of the Roman Empire, paving the way for an entrenched State church where power was centralized in the clergy and interwoven with government.[3] These hierarchical structures grew more complex and bureaucratic almost from the outset, obscuring even more the simple New Testament pattern. This trend continued and even compounded through the Middle Ages, and, as a consequence, the purpose and role of the biblical deacon was further marginalized. The Roman Catholic Church pulled deacons into the priesthood to perform ritualistic tasks, the reading of Scripture, and assisting priests at the altar.[4] As the Roman Empire fragmented, the church began to split over a variety of issues, essentially separating the church into two groups, Catholics and Eastern Orthodox Christians. Nevertheless, to this day both Rome and the Eastern Orthodox follow a hierarchical church leadership structure that has little resemblance to the true New Testament biblical structure.

It was not until the sixteenth century that the Reformation leaders challenged Catholic and Orthodox traditions and brought back much of the truth of Scripture, including leadership polity and structure. The Reformation brought a rebirth of scriptural clarity through a proper historical and grammatical view of biblical interpretation.[5] John Calvin led the charge in applying biblical clarity and biblical simplicity to church leadership structure that had been bloated and

---

[3] Cornelis Van Dam, *The Deacon: Biblical Foundations for Today's Ministry of Mercy* (Grand Rapids, MI: Reformation Heritage Books, 2016), 98-101.
[4] O'Donnell, *Handbook*, 14.
[5] Cliff McManis, *The Biblically-Driven Church* (Cupertino, CA: With All Wisdom Publications, 2016), 101-102.

compromised by the Roman Catholic Church. In Calvin's day, formal church leadership was totally corrupt, including the office of deacon. Of this institutionalized corruption he wrote, "in the present church...we shall find few or almost none whom the ancient canons would not have judged unworthy. If one was not a drunkard, he was a fornicator; if one was free from this vice, he was either a gambler or sportsman, or a loose liver."[6]

Calvin rightly bemoaned that "no one should assume a public office in the church without a call"(Heb 5:4).[7] With Calvin's pronouncements providing support, a goal of this book is to illuminate the true biblical model of New Testament church leadership, as seen in the simple yet elegant leadership structure Christ created—elders and deacons—with elders as the spiritual leaders shepherding the flock of Christ and deacons fulfilling the role of servant-leaders. Both are leaders over the church in their respective roles.

The Reformers launched the Protestant movement and focused on the New Testament elder-shepherding structure. But once again, a drift away from the biblical model occurred. In time, a host of denominations including the Lutherans, Presbyterians, Baptists, Methodists and others moved away from the New Testament structure. However, in the last 100 years, many Protestants have thrown off traditional

---

[6] John Calvin, *Institutes of the Christian Religion*, translated by Henry Beveridge (Peabody, MA: Hendrickson Publishers, 2008), IV.5.1.
[7] Calvin, *Institutes*, IV.3.9.

denominational structures and adopted non-denominational independence with a variety of church leadership structures.

Five Major Church Leadership Structures

Below are five major church leadership structures prominent today, along with a brief explanation of each structure's form of government and view on deacons. It will become clear that the views on the roles of elders and deacons are as diverse as they are distant from the true New Testament model.

Hierarchical-autocratic

This form of church leadership is practiced by Episcopalians, Anglicans, Eastern Orthodox, Roman Catholics, some Methodists, and some Lutherans.[8] Though the leadership model varies across the denominations, they all share the conviction that primary authority resides with the bishop. This view likens the office of bishop to the pattern purportedly established by the apostles. But unlike the teaching of the apostles, this is an autocratic system in which the bishop appoints leaders to local congregations; neither the local leadership nor its congregation has input in appointing their leaders. Above the bishops are other layers of clergy with regional and policy oversight.

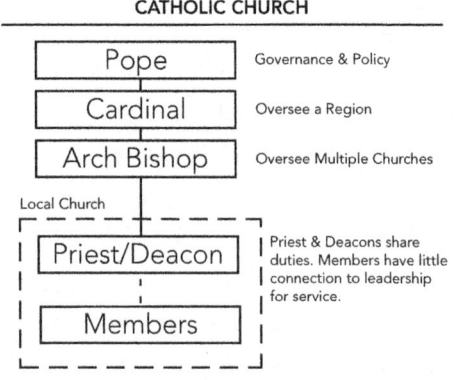

In the Roman Catholic Church, deacons are the lowest position among the clergy and can be either a full-time

---

[8] Benjamin L. Merkle, *40 Questions About Elders and Deacons* (Grand Rapids, MI: Kregel Publications, 2008), 26.

vocational position or part-time lay position.⁹ Their duties can include ministering communion, proclaiming the gospel during Mass, and counseling church members. Like Catholic deacons, Methodist deacons support the upper clergy (pastors), but unlike Catholic deacons, Methodist deacons also perform the duties performed by upper clergy including teaching, preaching, overseeing funerals and weddings, helping develop ministries, and counseling. Methodists believe deacons are called by God to serve in various capacities. They are, accordingly, trained and installed by upper clergy mostly to serve upper clergy in their duties.[10]

Hierarchical-representative or Reformed

This form of church leadership is used primarily by Presbyterian and other Reformed denominations.[11] This leadership structure is hierarchical, utilizing multiple levels of authority above the local church. There are four levels of elders/bishops: the Session (local church elders);

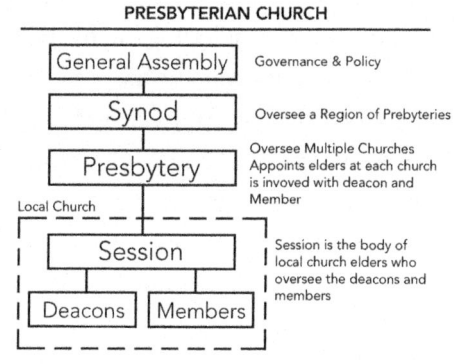

the Presbytery (elders/bishop overseeing multiple local churches); the Synod (bishops overseeing multiple Presbyteries); and the General Assembly (the highest governing body). This hierarchical structure is representative

---

⁹ "Catholic Priests – Hierarchy, Roles, and Requirements," Scripture Catholic, last modified 2022, https://www.scripturecatholic.com/catholic-priests/.
[10] "Deacons and Diaconal Ministers," Resource UMC, last modified 2018, https://www.resourceumc.org/en/content/deacons-and-diaconal-ministers.
[11] Merkle, *40 Questions*, 27.

because each local church's congregation and its elders select those who are in the hierarchical structure above them.

In Presbyterian leadership, deacons are charged with the ministry of mercy to show the love of Christ by providing for the poor and afflicted[12] as well as assisting the elders in pastoral care in a variety of ways. Or as *The Book of Order* puts it, the office of deacon is one of "sympathy, witness, and service."[13] As a formal group, Presbyterian deacons comprise a "board." Presbyterian deacons can assist with the Lord's Supper, manage the church money, lead worship, visit the sick, welcome new members or take on any other special tasks as directed by the Session.

Local-representative or congregationalism
This form of leadership structure is used by several denominations including many Baptist denominations, some Lutheran denominations, as well as Congregational, independent, and Bible churches. These churches are highly representative. They champion local congregational democracy and independence. The authority of the church lies with the majority vote of the assembly of believers.[14] These churches have two offices: elder(s)/pastor(s) and deacon(s). But the ultimate authority is vested in the congregation. Individual church autonomy is highly regarded by churches with this form of leadership. This local autonomy is supported by the denomination's administrative structure which offers support and resources to the local churches but does not have a hierarchal structure.

---

[12] Van Dam, *The Deacon*, xi.
[13] Earl S. Johnson, Jr., "The Presbyterian Deacon," *The Presbyterian Outlook*, August 31, 2008.
[14] Merkle, *40 Questions*, 27-28.

REPERSENTATIVE CHURCH STRUCTURES

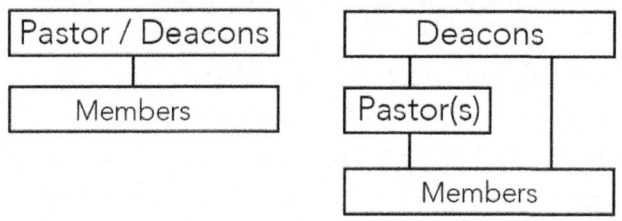

BAPTIST CHURCH STRUCTURES

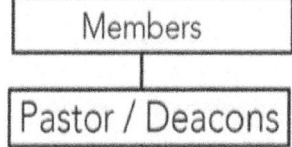

Usually a single (senior) pastor and multiple deacons where deacons have shepherding duties. Deacons may or may not be able to remove a pastor. Church membership can remove a pastor or deacon.

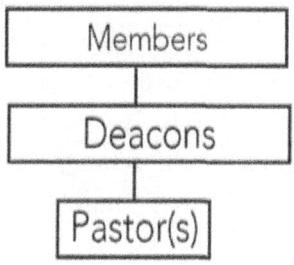

Usually a single (senior) pastor (but can have multiple pastors) and multiple deacons where deacons have shepherding duties with a corporate committee structure and oversight of the pastor. Both pastor and deacons work with the members and both pastor and deacons are removed by the members.

The autonomy of these churches leads to a variety of views on the roles of deacons. The Baptists are especially wide ranging in their views. Below are three differing Baptistic viewpoints:

1. <u>Blurred Responsibilities with Elders</u> - According to this view, in addition to service, deacons play a role as spiritual leaders of the church. Operating under the belief that part of the deacon's role is to teach and guide members of the church body, churches with this viewpoint see the deacon as essential in areas of pastoral leadership. This is a blurring of the New Testament roles of elders and deacons.

2. <u>Deacons are Shepherds</u> - Many Baptist churches believe deacons are shepherds.[15] These churches see deacons not as equals to the role of an elder/pastor but, rather, as working in partnership with the elder/pastor. In other words, the deacon's duties are primarily in the realm of pastoral leadership.[16] Beyond blurring traditional lines, these Baptists believe deacons can be preaching, teaching, and counseling just as the pastor/elder does. Churches with this form of leadership see the pastor as the one who gives the vision and direction of the church. The pastor, with the deacons, then operate together to lead the congregation in that vision. Howard B. Foshee, in his book, *Now That You're a Deacon,* attempts to explain this shared view of leadership by offering an initial, general statement of pastoral leadership: "As a generalist leader the pastor leads the church to determine its spiritual mission. A pastor succeeds as a leader when he guides the church toward the attainment of its priority goals."[17] Foshee initially states that deacons are

---

[15] Howard B. Foshee, *Now That You're a Deacon* (Nashville, TN: B&H Publishing Group, 1975), 15-16.
[16] Robert Naylor, *The Baptist Deacon* (Nashville, TN: Broadman and Holman Publishers, 1955), 10.
[17] Foshee, *Now That You're a Deacon,* 27-28.

shepherds, only to contradict himself by later stating that deacons serve behind the scenes. His winding explanation goes on to assert that deacon leadership is in harmony with the idea stated by an ancient Chinese philosopher—namely, that a leader is best when people barely know that he exists, not so good when people obey and acclaim him, and worse when they despise him. This curious analogy with a humanistic ideal continues: "Fail to honor people, they fail to honor you, but a good leader who talks little, when his work is finished, they will say, we did this ourselves."[18]

So Foshee not only contradicts himself, but he also uses an inconsistent example to explain a deacon's humble work. According to Foshee a deacon should not be leading by example or be a model for others to follow. Rather, it "is best when people barely know he exists; if the deacon is successful, people never know that they have been led." What is more troublesome, is that Foshee does not quote Christ, Paul, or any biblical reference, but rather a pagan Chinese philosopher.

3. <u>Changing Landscape of Traditional Congregational Baptist Churches</u> - These churches traditionally have a single elder/pastor and multiple deacons that often operate like a corporate board of directors overseeing all church operations and finance. A few congregational churches have moved to multiple elders and multiple deacons. These churches govern themselves by using a hybrid between elder shepherding and traditional Congregationalism. These hybrid Congregationalist churches believe the role of deacon is strictly a servant role, with all teaching, preaching, and spiritual leadership coming from the elders. However, the congregation has ultimate

---

[18] Foshee, *Now That You're a Deacon*, 28. Foshee's "invisible leader" notion is in direct conflict with Scripture which commands leaders to "be an example" to the believers (1 Tim 4:12), which can only happen with public, visible service.

authority in many areas by voting on topics such as the budget, leaders, church discipline, new hires and more.

Egalitarian

This form of leadership structure is used mostly by Brethren and Quaker congregations and a growing number of those in the "house-church" movement. These churches minimize the need for a formal leadership structure and prefer an organic, free-flowing dynamic as—in their words—the Holy Spirit leads.

EGALITARIAN CHURCH

Elders	Deacons	Members

Elders will organize but not assert true headship over the body. Everyone is allowed to teach

These churches stress the priesthood of all believers as the guiding principle. These churches may have a pastor, but teaching and preaching is not limited to the pastor. They have the freedom to let the Holy Spirit prompt others to share God's Word, many times during the church service in a spontaneous manner.[19]

Quaker churches do not have deacons. Deacons in Brethren churches focus on caregiving ministries to individuals and families in the areas of welcoming, nurturing, reconciling, and witnessing to both the church body and those outside the church.[20]

New Testament elder-shepherding

There are evangelical churches, independent nondenominational churches, and even some denominational churches that hold to the first century roles of deacons as taught in the New Testament. In these churches elders are the spiritual overseers of the local church (Heb 13:17; 1 Pet 5:1-4).

---

[19] Merkle, *40 Questions*, 28.
[20] "Deacon Ministry," Church of the Brethren, last modified 2022, https://www.brethren.org/discipleshipmin/deacons/.

There is no hierarchy above them. The elders oversee the ministry of the Word and are responsible for the teaching, preaching, and counseling within their congregation. Elders do not have to be the *only* ones who teach, preach, and counsel, but are responsible for vetting all that do. Elders are also responsible for the operations and finance of the church with affirmation from the congregation (see Acts 4:35).

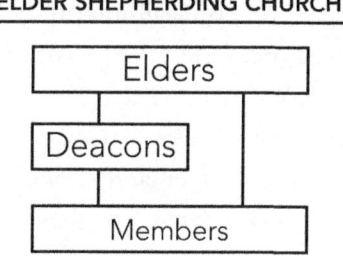

Deacons are seen only in roles of service. In his book, *Paul's Vision for the Deacons*, Alexander Strauch notes, "deacons are not a separate autonomous body of offi-cials disconnected from the body of overseers. Deacons operate under the leadership of the elders."[21] They serve under the guidance of the elders in roles of service to and for the church. They complement the ministry of the elders, freeing them to focus on the ministry of the Word and prayer.

In addition to these five leadership structures, there are countless churches that disregard the need for the office of deacon as mandated in the New Testament. In *Confident Pastoral Leadership*, for example, two popular church leaders tell their readers that we cannot be confident in what the Bible says about church leadership structure. These church leaders erroneously allege, "Whereas the foundational doctrines of our Christian faith are clearly defined in the Scriptures, there is no clear definition and picture given for the official organization

---

[21] Alexander Strauch, *Paul's Vision for the Deacons* (Littleton, CO: Lewis and Roth Publishers, 2017), 57.

of the church on a local or aggregate basis."[22] In other words, they say the sufficient and perspicuous Bible is not adequate or clear on the all-important matter of church leadership structure. One of the most famous pastors of the modern era, Rick Warren, has a similar view. In his book on ecclesiology, *The Purpose Driven Church*, Warren completely ignores the offices of elder and deacon and neglects any discussion of passages related to these essential positions that Christ appointed to lead and serve his church. Now churches whose leaders have imbibed Warren's view may or may not have ordained elders or deacons as part of their leadership structure. Nevertheless, the critical issue is that they now don't think elders and deacons are *essential*. Instead of looking to the Bible's clear instruction on the subject of elder and deacon roles, these churches have chosen to rely on human wisdom in creating church leadership structures.

Summary

As time progressed and the church moved out of the apostolic era, what was a simple leadership structure in the first century with two offices (elders, focused on the ministry of the Word, and deacons serving the body through the direction of the elders) grew into an unbiblical and often unwieldy hierarchical structure. Then came the Reformation that, while denouncing these unbiblical leadership structures, spawned various "new" denominations that eventually repeated history by establishing man-made church leadership structures.

It is not surprising that with the five major church leadership structures coming from a mix of theological views, all with varying interpretations of Scripture, there is no

---

[22] Howard Sugden and Warren Wiersbe, *Confident Pastoral Leadership* (Chicago, IL: Moody Press, 1973), 42.

singular, cohesive view of the purpose and role of a deacon that comes anywhere close to being the mainstream Christian position. The fact is there are more views on the role and purpose of deacons than there are of church leadership structure. It is surprising that with only a few passages about this office, two millennia of church history, and endless scholarship that has been written on ecclesiology, there is not more agreement. It is sad to see that after two thousand years Christ's church remains so confused regarding its leadership. Christ gave specific instructions to the apostles on the structure of church leadership but as is too often the case, we have taken it upon ourselves to reframe and remake that simple structure laid out in Scripture. Now we have what can only be described as a convoluted mess regarding church leadership, especially when it comes to the polity of deacons. This sad circumstance, in turn, puts at risk countless congregations that unquestioningly follow leaders who do not use and teach the biblical role of deacon.

After having explained why so many churches do not follow the New Testament leadership structure, the next four chapters of this book are dedicated to setting forth the biblical foundation for the deacon's role. The next chapter will present the origin and usage of the word for "deacon" in its proper context.

"To all the saints in Christ Jesus who are at Philippi, with the overseers and **deacons**."
Philippians 1:1

"I know your works, your love and faith and **service** and patient endurance, and that your latter works exceed the first."
Revelations 2:19

"…just as you learned it from Epaphras, our beloved fellow bond servant, who is a faithful **minister** of Christ."
Colossians 1:7

3

The Meaning of "Deacon"

To understand the biblical position of deacon, we must start with its meaning and usage throughout the New Testament.

There are three Greek words used in the New Testament that come from the root-word *daikon-*. Two of these words are nouns: *diakonos* (masculine), and *diakonia* (feminine). One word is a verb: *diakoneo* and it "has the special quality of indicating very personally the service rendered to others."[1] These three words occur exactly 100 times in the New Testament. Depending on the English Bible translation, they are translated as "deacon," "servant," "helper," "minister," or other similar terms. The apostle Paul embraced this simple term, which in its root means "to serve," and transformed it into a technical title for the second office of the church. As we embark on studying the etymology of the word "deacon," it is good to remember that Greek nouns can have masculine, feminine, and neuter forms. With this in mind, below is the breakdown of the 100 times the various Greek versions of the root-word

---

[1] Gerhard Kittle, ed., *Theological Dictionary of the New Testament*, Vol. II (Grand Rapids, MI: Eerdmans Publishing Co., 1964), 81.

daikon- are used, as well as their translation in the English Standard Version (ESV).

Diakonos (διάκονος pronounced *dee-ak'-on-os*, noun, masculine)
Paul used the noun form *diakonos* to create the formal title for the office of deacon. That word, in the context of the office of deacon, is used three times in Scripture: 1 Timothy 3:8; 1 Timothy 3:12, and Philippians 1:1. In other words, Paul outlines the office of deacon (1 Tim 3:8, 12) and then uses it only one other time (Phil 1:1).

The twenty-six other passages that use *diakonos* do not refer to the formal office. This usage is made clear by the context of the passage. When the generic use of *diakonos* is used to describe a person, it is translated "minister" or "servant." Below are some examples.

Paul referring to himself
- Ephesians 3:7 – "Of this gospel I was made a **minister** according to the gift of God's grace, which was given me by the working of his power."

Paul describing Tychicus, Timothy, and Epaphras
- Ephesians 6:21 – "So that you also may know how I am and what I am doing, Tychicus the beloved brother and faithful **minister** in the Lord will tell you everything."
- 1 Timothy 4:6 – "If you put these things before the brothers, you will be a good **servant** of Christ Jesus, being trained in the words of the faith and of the good doctrine that you have followed."
- Colossians 1:7 – "just as you learned it from Epaphras, our beloved fellow bond servant, who is a faithful **minister** of Christ."

Other examples of diakonos
- Matthew 22:13 – "Then the king said to the **attendants**" (a simple servant to the king).
- Romans 13:4 – "For he is the **servant** of God" (secular rulers and authorities in government).
- Romans 15:8 – "For I tell you that Christ became a **servant**" (Christ as a servant to Israel).
- 2 Corinthians 3:6 – "who has made us sufficient to be **ministers** of a new covenant" (all believers are ministers of the gospel).
- 2 Corinthians 11:15 – "So it is no surprise if his **servants**" (these disguised servants were followers of Satan).

The Twenty-Nine Uses of *Diakonos*

Title of the Office
    Philippians 1:1; 1 Timothy 3:8, 12

Servant, Minister, Co-Worker
    Matthew 20:26; 22:13; 23:11
    Mark 9:35; 10:43
    John 2:5; 2:9; 12:26
    Romans 13:4 (twice); 15:8; 16:1
    1 Corinthians 3:5
    2 Corinthians 3:6; 6:4; 11:15 (twice); 11:23
    Galatians 2:17
    Ephesians 3:7; 6:21

Diakonia (διακονία pronounced *dee-ak-on-ee'-ah*, noun, feminine)
A feminine noun used thirty-four times, describing the service of Christian love by those caring for and ministering to others. In the ESV, this word is translated as "ministry," "serve," "service "or "serving," and "relief." This word was used by

Luke, Paul, the author of Hebrews, and John.

- Luke 10:40
- Acts 1:17; 1:25; 6:1; 6:4; 11:29; 12:25; 20:24; 21:19
- Romans 11:13; 12:7 (twice); 15:31
- 1 Corinthians 12:5; 16:15
- 2 Corinthians 3:7; 3:8; 3:9 (twice); 4:1, 5:18; 6:3; 8:4; 9:1; 9:12; 9:13; 11:8
- Ephesians 4:12
- Colossians 4:17
- 1 Timothy 1:12
- 2 Timothy 4:5; 4:11
- Hebrews 1:14
- Revelation 2:19

Diakoneo (διακονέω pronounced *dee-ak-on-eh'-o*, verb)
A verb used thirty-seven times, primarily referring to the task of serving, ministering, and helping other people. In the ESV it is translated as "serve," "minister," "administered," "help" and "support." The word is used by Matthew, Mark, Luke, John, Paul, the writer of Hebrews, and Peter.

- Mathew 4:11; 8:15; 20:28 (twice); 25:44; 27:55
- Mark 1:13; 1:31; 10:45 (twice); 15:41
- Luke 4:39, 8:3; 10:40, 12:37, 17:8; 22:26; 22:27 (twice)
- John 12:2; 12:26 (twice)
- Acts 6:2; 19:22
- Romans 15:25
- 2 Corinthians 3:3; 8:19; 8:20
- 1 Timothy 3:10; 3:13
- 2 Timothy 1:18

- Philemon 13
- Hebrews 6:10 (twice)
- 1 Peter 1:12; 4:10; 4:11

Context Matters

As important as the word study of "deacon" is, each word's meaning can only be determined from its immediate context. Historically, six passages have been considered foundational in defining the position of deacon. We will begin with a quick review of the contextual setting of each passage: Acts 6:1-6; 1 Timothy 3:8-13; Philippians 1:1; Romans 16:1-15; 1 Timothy 2:9-10; and 1 Timothy 5:9-13.

Acts 6:1-6

In the first church in Jerusalem the apostles ordained seven men to care specifically for the widows in the congregation. This assignment came thirty years before the apostle Paul universalized the office of deacon. There are many parallels to the qualifications and roles of the seven in Acts 6 and the formal qualifications provided by Paul. *Diakoneo*, the verb form of deacon is used to describe the service to the widows. Because of these items, this passage is critical in the understanding of deacons. We will discuss this passage at length in chapters four, five, and six.

1 Timothy 3:8-13

Paul universalized the office of deacon by listing qualifications of a deacon, a deacon's duties, and the processes utilized to select and install deacons. First Timothy 3:8-13 is the foundational passage. These verses are essential to the study of a deacon's position and his role with a church, and therefore this passage will be thoroughly reviewed.

Philippians 1:1

Paul wrote Philippians probably while under house arrest in Rome around 62 AD (Acts 28:14-31),[2] prior to writing his first letter to Timothy, which he composed in 64-66 AD.[3] Paul starts the book of Philippians with a greeting: "To all the saints in Christ Jesus who are at Philippi, with the overseers and deacons" (Phil 1:1). There is no formal teaching about deacons in the passage; rather, this salutation is merely a simple identification of the church which Paul planted, along with a specific callout of the leadership roles within that church.

Romans 16:1-15

Paul wrote Romans while in Corinth between AD 55 and 58.[4] He concludes his letter to the Romans by recognizing several "servants." Some were specific servants of the church, while others were personally helpful to Paul. The context of the passage is Paul's personal greeting; he is not offering his instruction or commands. So, this passage does not teach specifically on the roles, purpose, or ministry of a deacon. The question is whether Paul is using the formal title of deacon to describe Phoebe. This passage has presented a challenge for Bible translators who have translated this word into English variously as "servant," "minister," "deacon" and "deaconess." The vast majority of scholars agree that 1 Timothy 3:8, 12 and Philippians 1:1 are the passages where Paul specifically addresses the formal office of deacon with Romans 16:1 being in question. The Philippians 1:1 passage is a general greeting to all the elders and deacons of the Philippian church. There are other places like Acts 15 and 20 where Paul provides a general address to elders but he does not recognize them by name. No

---

[2] H.C.G. Moule, *Studies in Philippians* (Grand Rapids, MI: Kregel Publications, 1977), 14.
[3] Norman L. Geisler, *A Popular Survey of the New Testament* (Ada, MI: Baker Books, 2007), 235.
[4] Thomas R. Schreiner, *Romans* (Grand Rapids, MI: Baker Academic, 2018), 3.

place across his epistles does Paul attribute the title of elder or deacon to a specific person. Epaphras in Colossians 1:7 is call by Paul *diakonos*—just as Phoebe—connected to a local church but translated minister.[5] If Paul was recognizing Phoebe as a formal deacon it would be the first time he did so for either of the formal offices. Contextually this is one reason Romans 16:1 is better translated as either "servant" or "minister." A fuller discussion of Phoebe and the context of the Romans 16:1 passage is in chapter eight.

1 Timothy 5:9-10 and 1 Timothy 2:9-10

1 Timothy 5:9-10 is commonly referred to as the "order of widows" from which the position of deaconess emerged.[6] The rationale is that 1 Timothy 2:9-10 establishes women for "works" of the church that are then outlined in vv. 9-10:

> [L]ikewise also that women should adorn themselves in respectable apparel, with modesty and self-control, not with braided hair and gold or pearls or costly attire, but with what is proper for women who profess godliness—**with good works** (1 Tim 2:9-10).
>
> **Let a widow be enrolled** if she is not less than sixty

---

[5] *The NET Bible* notes on Romans 16:1; "It is debated whether διάκονος here refers to a specific office within the church. One contextual argument used to support this view is that Phoebe is associated with a particular church, Cenchrea, and as such would therefore be a deacon of that church. In the NT some who are called διάκονος are related to a particular church, yet the scholarship consensus is that such individuals are not deacons but 'servants' or 'ministers' (other viable translations for διάκονος). For example, Epaphras is associated with the church in Colossians and is called a διάκονος in Col 1:7 but no contemporary translation regards him as a deacon. In 1 Tim 4:6 Paul calls Timothy διάκονος; Timothy was associated with the church in Ephesus, but he obviously was not a deacon. In addition, the lexical evidence leans away from this view: Within the NT, the διάκονος word group rarely functions with a technical nuance. In any case the evidence is not compelling either way. The view accepted in the translation above is that Phoebe was a servant of the church not a deaconess although this conclusion should be regarded as tentative," *The NET Bible: New English Translation* (Thomas Nelson, 2019), 2183.

[6] Christina Hip-Flores, "Consecrated Widows: A Restored Ancient Vocation in the Catholic Church," *Logos: A Journal of Catholic Thought and Culture* 22, *no. 1* (Winter 2019), 108.

years of age, having been the wife of one husband, and having a reputation for good works: if she has brought up children, has shown hospitality, has washed the feet of the saints, has cared for the afflicted, and **has devoted herself to every good work** (1 Tim 5:9-13).

In April 2020 Pope Francis established a new commission to study a potential formal position of women deacons in the Catholic Church based on these passages as well as church tradition.[7] There are two contextual problems for using these passages to establish the formal position of women deacons. First, neither passage is in the context of church leadership. In 1 Timothy 2, Paul is giving instruction on worship, and in 1 Timothy 5 Paul gives instructions on older men, widows, and elders. Second, there is no form of *diakon* used in these passages. So, these two passages are wonderful examples of the love and good deeds we are to show one another,[8] but they are not instructions on church leadership or directions for church deacons. It is illegitimate to consider these passages as applicable to church leadership or the deacon role because the primary noun used to describe the formal office of deacons is missing. Given these contextual issues, 1 Timothy 2:9-10 and

---

[7] Sr Bernadette Mary Rei, "Pope Institutes New Commission to Study Women Deacons," *Vatican News*, April 8, 2020, https://www.vaticannews.va/en/pope/news/2020-04/pope-commission-women-deacons.html.

[8] There are over forty "one anothers" in Scripture based on Christ's new command given the night before His death in John 13:34-35: *"A new commandment I give to you, that you love one another, even as I have loved you, that you also love one another. By this all men will know that you are my disciples, if you have love for one another."* Christ urged them to love as He had loved them: to have a mindset of love, to act in love, and to think in love toward one another. He had a mindset of love toward us even when we did not show it toward Him. Christ taught the disciples to think and act in love, with His sacrificial death being the ultimate example.

1 Timothy 5:9-13 therefore cannot be considered in the study of the office of deacon.

Summary

Most of the New Testament authors used at least one form of *daikon-* to describe either people or actions in the 100 occurrences of the word. In Paul's case, *diakonos* is the form of the word used by Paul to universalize the office, and the word appears only three times in noun form when describing or addressing the formal office of deacon (1 Tim 3:8, 12; Phil 1:1).

Beyond the conclusion coming from a word study of *daikon-*, the *context* of the six identified deacon passages eliminates 1 Timothy 2:9-10 and 1 Timothy 5:9-13 from consideration in our search for a true, biblically sourced definition of a deacon's role. Instead, as we have seen, 1 Timothy 3:8-13 and Acts 6:1-6 are foundational for studying the office of deacon. In Acts 6 the apostles inaugurated the use of the word "servant" to designate a collection of men to assist them in their duties. Thirty years later, Paul universalized the office of deacon in his first letter to Timothy. Finally, Philippians 1:1 and Romans 16:1 are needed to fully understand the office of deacon. Chapters 4 and 8 will look more at the context surrounding these verses. But next, we turn to look at the history of deacons in the New Testament.

"Now in the days when the disciples were increasing in number, [in the immediate years following Christ's resurrection and ascension,] a complaint by the Hellenists arose against the Hebrews because the former's widows were being neglected in the daily distribution. In response, the twelve Apostles summoned the full number of the disciples and said, "It is not right that we should give up preaching the word of God to serve tables. Therefore, brothers, pick out from among you seven men of good repute, full of the Spirit and of wisdom, whom we will appoint to this duty. But we will devote ourselves to prayer and to the ministry of the word." And what they said pleased the whole gathering, and they chose Stephen, a man full of faith and of the Holy Spirit, and Philip, and Prochorus, and Nicanor, and Timon, and Parmenas, and Nicolaus, a proselyte of Antioch. These they set before the apostles, and they prayed and laid their hands on them. And the word of God continued to increase, and the number of the disciples multiplied greatly in Jerusalem."
Acts 6:1-7

"Deacons likewise must be dignified, not double-tongued, not addicted to much wine, not greedy for dishonest gain. They must hold the mystery of the faith with a clear conscience. And let them also be tested first; then let them serve as deacons if they prove themselves blameless. Their wives likewise must be dignified, not slanderers, but sober-minded, faithful in all things. Let deacons each be the husband of one wife, managing their children and their own households well. For those who serve well as deacons gain a good standing for themselves and also great confidence in the faith that is in Christ Jesus."
1 Timothy 3:8-13

4

From Acts 6 to 1 Timothy 3

In the last chapter we established Acts 6 and 1 Timothy 3 are the two foundational passages in the Bible that provide information on the role of deacons. The events of Acts 6 occurred somewhere around 35 AD.[1] Paul wrote 1 Timothy after his three-year stay in Ephesus sometime between 64-66 AD. There are, therefore, approximately thirty years between the events of Acts 6 and 1 Timothy 3.

Nevertheless, there is a debate as to whether the seven men chosen in Acts 6 were the deacons of Christ's church. Below are the major views:

> *Not Deacons*
> Neither in Acts 6 nor anywhere else in Acts are the seven called deacons. If the apostles were establishing an office in Acts 6, it is strange that these seven are not referred to as deacons. There are several places in Acts that elders are mentioned (11:30; 14:23; 15:20), but deacons are never mentioned. The seven men were chosen for a specific task, and, as the preceding paragraphs have determined, these men were not

---

[1] Merrill F. Unger, *The New Unger's Bible Dictionary* (Chicago, IL: Moody Publishers, 2006), 968.

deacons though their function of serving is similar to that of deacons.²

Prototype of Deacons
Though the noun forms of deacon are not used in Acts 6, the verb *diakoneo* does occur in the Acts 6:2 text. Furthermore, church elders were not yet established at the time of Acts 6. The seven men did assist the apostles, just as deacons are to assist the elders as set forth in 1 Timothy 3. Acts 6 nevertheless does provide a pattern that was continued in the early church.³

The First Deacons
When all factors had been considered, the congregation chose seven men as instructed by the apostles. The apostles ordained them for the role and, thereby, a new office was instituted in the church. Later in Scripture, Paul gives this office the formal title of deacon. This has been the position of the Christian church since the second century.⁴

In this chapter we are going to see that the apostles who walked with Christ during his three-year ministry later ordained men for service after Jesus ascended to heaven. Paul, who became an apostle on the road to Damascus, followed the same framework established by the apostles thirty years earlier when he added more specific qualifications, formalized the selection process and, of course, gave a title to the office. What the

---

[2] John MacArthur, *The MacArthur New Testament Commentary: 1 Timothy* (Chicago, IL: Moody Publishers, 1995), xiv.
[3] Benjamin Merkle, *40 Questions About Elders and Deacons* (Grand Rapids, MI: Kregel Publications, 2008), 227.
[4] Cornelis Van Dam, *The Deacon: Biblical Foundations for Today's Ministry of Mercy* (Grand Rapids, MI: Reformation Heritage Books, 2016), 51.

apostles established in Acts 6—a formalized group of servant-men with qualifications—thus was advanced by Paul in a similar manner in 1 Timothy 3:8-13.

Regardless of which of the above views one espouses, it is clear that Paul did not redefine what was done in Acts 6. Rather, he used the same framework and provided more information. Although the seven men are not formally called *diakonos* in Acts 6, we will see that the purpose of the position, the qualifications required for it, the alignment of leadership, and the seriousness of the position are similar to that of the office of deacon that Paul universalized in his first letter to Timothy. We conclude, therefore, that Acts 6 needs to be a part of the scriptural data in our analysis of deacons.

Acts 6:1-7

Soon after the death of Christ, the Jerusalem church began to grow quickly, with 3,000 added on just the first day (Acts 2:41), with the Lord continuing to add "to their number day by day" (Acts 2:47). Soon, this first church grew to "about five thousand" (Acts 4:4). If you add women and children, the church likely had more than 10,000 people. After this experience of immediate and explosive response to the gospel, the growth continued: "all the more believers in the Lord, multitudes of men and women, were constantly added to their number" (Acts 5:14). This was a full-blown mega-church with thousands of people but there were only twelve apostles at the helm, serving as the shepherds of the church.

The needs and demands of this enormous group of believers were no doubt a logistical challenge if not a nightmare for the small group of leaders. Not everyone's needs could possibly be met, and this soon became readily apparent in Acts 6. In verse 1, a complaint came to the apostles that the Jewish widows were being favored over the Greek widows in the daily distribution of the food. The apostles knew this was a serious issue. It was either something as simple as favoritism that had gotten out of hand, or it was something worse such as racism, a divisive sin. We don't know the root issue because the Bible does not say what it was. Either way, the apostles' response was significant and decisive. The apostles were the spiritual leaders of a mega-church, and they knew they could not set aside the ministry of teaching and preaching the Word to do basic service work. At the same time, the root of this issue was serious, and it needed solid spiritual men of integrity and character to manage it.

The apostles determined this was a sizable and significant issue. Their response was just as sizable and significant, and it included five major elements.

1. *The apostles diagnosed the problem* – v. 1: "a complaint... widows were being neglected."
   Complaints in church (wherever there are large groups of people, believers or not) are common. It is reasonable to assume this was not the first complaint of the new church in Jerusalem. However, it is the first complaint recorded in Scripture and one the apostles determined was legitimate and necessary to address. Instead of trying to manage the problem which they determined would consume a significant portion of time ("...it is not right that we give up preaching the word of God to serve tables," v. 2) they decided to appoint others to the task.

2. *The apostles took the initiative* – v. 3c: "whom we will appoint to this duty."

There were several possible solutions available to the apostles. They could have simply dictated how distribution was to be done. They could have directly assigned leaders to manage the distribution. They could have gathered those who were already doing the distribution and given encouragement to them to do it with the love of Christ. The Holy Spirit led the apostles to determine this was much more than simple logistical management. Spiritually strong men that were respected by the people were needed to address this issue. After all, this was a ministry to widows, vulnerable women who needed care. All eyes were watching. This may be the reason part of the initiative the apostles took was to include the community in selecting the men.

The apostles determined the number of men it would take to address this issue. The fact they chose seven tells us the issue was sizable. The Bible does not give the apostles' reasoning for the number, but the very fact that it would take seven men to address the food distribution is intriguing, and it could answer the question of why the apostles themselves did not have the bandwidth to be directly involved since there were only twelve of them. So, the apostles chose how to manage the problem, and as part of that management was to determine the number of men it would take to handle the task.

3. *The apostles communicated the purpose, plan and process to the community* – v. 2: "and the twelve summoned the full number of the disciples and said…".

The apostles gathered the community to communicate their plan, how the community would be involved and make clear the purpose. Their time could not be spent away from the priorities of shepherding and ministry of the Word. They instead chose to select a group of men dedicated to managing the issue for them.

The apostles established a simple selection process for the seven men that involved the community. But it is important to note that the apostles oversaw each step and then reviewed and approved of the men who were selected. "It is not right that we should give up preaching the word of God to serve tables. Therefore, brothers, pick out from among you seven men...whom we will appoint to this duty" (vv. 2b-3).

In other words, the apostles instructed the community to select seven men. This was a delegated task. This was not the apostles turning over the process to the congregation like many believe. As part of their instruction, the apostles set forth the qualifications of the men the community was to select: "men of good repute, full of the Spirit and of wisdom" (v. 3).

The community of believers were given instructions to find men that met specific qualifications; men of solid character and integrity; men who have shown they are led by the Spirit, exemplifying Christ in their attitudes and actions; men who demonstrate godly wisdom, not double-minded, and who don't wrestle with being pulled between the Word and the world; and men who live by faith and not by sight. These were then to be set before the apostles (Acts 6:6a).

An additional note on the apostles including the community of believers in the selection process is pertinent. The Old Testament did not use representative government. Leaders were primarily selected by God through other leaders and appointed to their positions. There were a few occasions in the Bible where God had his people choose their leaders, but that was only in specific situations and not the standard circumstance (King Saul, 1 Samuel 10; Jeroboam, 1 Kings 11). Christ was making a change here, for the sake of his church and in correspondence with the New Covenant reality of the Holy Spirit dwelling in every believer by establishing a process of involving the whole community of believers in the selection of its leaders. In the New Covenant, *every* Christian is a priest, not just the descendants of Aaron as in the Old Covenant (cf. 1 Pet 2:9).

4. *The apostles examined the seven* – "These they set before the apostles" (Acts 6:6a).
   Verses 3c and 6a confirm the fact that the apostles delegated the initial selection of the seven men. That is the only portion of the selection process that was delegated. Verse 6a clearly shows that the selected men were to be presented to the apostles who would then confirm each candidate's qualifications before appointing him to the task. Below are four translations of verse Acts 6:6a:

   > NKJV – "whom they **set before** the apostles; and when they had prayed, they laid hands on them."

ESV – "These they **set before** the apostles, and they prayed and laid their hands on them."

NASB – "And these they **brought before** the apostles; and after praying, they laid their hands on them."

CSB – "They had them **stand before** the apostles, who prayed and laid their hands on them."

All four translations are slightly different. Isolated from the context they do not capture the fullness of the event, but collectively they begin to approach a more accurate rendering of the original. The Greek words *histemi enopion*—translated above as "set before," "brought before," or "stand before"—are word-for-word accurate. The implication is that this was a public and corporate process of evaluation. After vetting men based on specific objective qualifications the congregation set these men before the apostles for formal confirmation. They were further examined by the apostles. This is similar to what one encounters in reading Matthew 27:11, where Jesus "stood before" Pilate. Matthew captures this idea of the public scrutiny or being "further examined" by Pilate as he questions Christ. Here in Acts it is the same. The seven men were brought before the apostles after being chosen by the community. The apostles did not simply approve them because they were selected by the community. If that had been the case, then it would be the community "appointing them," but 6:3 is clear that the apostles did the appointing. Seven men were initially selected by the community *then* brought before the apostles for further examination and final approval.

The apostles thus oversaw the selection of the seven: they established the number of men to be chosen, the selection process, and the qualifications. And the selection process included their examination to affirm God's will.

5. *The apostles laid hands on the seven* – "they prayed and laid hands on them" (v. 6b).
After their examination the apostles prayed and laid hands on them. There are several words in Greek that are translated "prayer" in English. One refers to making a request; another is an intercession. The word here, *proseuchomai*, is an earnest prayer.[5] In this case the apostles were praying in earnest to seek and affirm God's will. It is clear, therefore, that the apostles were not just going to approve any man set before them for this important task.

The laying on of hands is the public acknowledgement, by both leadership and community, of the men being launched into ministry. Today, we use the term "ordination." Technically, there is no New Testament Greek word that directly corresponds to our English word "ordination."

---

[5] Walter Bauer, *A Greek-English Lexicon of the New Testament and Other Early Christian Literature* (Chicago, IL: University of Chicago Press, 2001), 713. It was the apostles who laid hands on the seven for prayer, not the congregation (contra. Clean Rogers, Jr.), for it was the apostles who "ratified the choice (verse 3); cf. A. T. Robertson, *Word Picture in the New Testament, Vol. III* (Grand Rapids, MI: Baker Book House, 1930), 74.

So, what were the seven being ordained into? It is clear by the context of the passage that they were being chosen to a specific task of serving. Twice in the passage, in verses 2 and 4, it is emphasized that the apostles needed to stay concentrated on the ministry of the Word, implying that these men will be appointed to serve.

The apostles were not laying hands on men to help in the ministry of the Word. The apostles determined to have men specifically chosen to *serve* in the managing of specific tasks. The apostles' laying hands on the seven men was vital in demonstrating to the community the seriousness of the position and the need for men to serve in the carrying out of specific tasks.

To recap, when the young church of Acts came across its first major issue that the apostles determined required a special group of servants, they involved the community in the selection of leaders. The church, therefore, set a precedent that continues to this day, which entails the saints' involvement.

The apostles took specific steps:
1. Diagnosed the problem: they heard the complaint, realized the size and weight of the issue and determined to act.
2. Took initiative: determined the solution was to lay hands on a group of qualified godly men to manage the issue and involve the community for the initial selection.
3. Communicated the purpose, plan, and process: they communicated to the community the

purpose of creating a new level of leadership and the plan and process for implementation.
4. Examined the candidates: after the community made an initial selection of seven men that met the qualifications established by the apostles, the apostles then examined the men.
5. Ordained the seven: after approving the seven selected by the community, the apostles prayed and ordained them into service.

This process was planned by Christ and implemented by men through the power of the Holy Spirit as can be seen from verse 7: "and the word of God continued to increase, and the number of the disciples multiplied greatly in Jerusalem."

Next, we turn to 1 Timothy 3:8-13, where Paul universalized the office of deacon.

1 Timothy 3:8-13

Approximately thirty years after the events of Acts 6, Paul writes Timothy while in Macedonia. First Timothy is the first of Paul's pastoral letters, the other two being his second letter to Timothy and Titus. Timothy was a young pastor. Since being released from prison in Rome, Paul had recently visited Timothy and the church in Ephesus. In 1 Timothy, Paul wrote to provide instructions on how Timothy should "conduct himself in the house of God" (1 Tim 3:15), providing details to Timothy on public worship, a pastor's personal life, how to confront sin in the church, the care of widows, how to handle money, and establishing church leadership with elders and deacons.

Although the terms "elder" and "deacon" are not used in Acts 6, one can readily see that the leadership framework in Acts 6 and 1 Timothy 3 is essentially parallel. In fact, during the first thirty years of church history that started with a single church in Jerusalem and grew into many churches throughout most of the Roman world, the leadership framework never changed.

Leadership Framework

The church management structure, headship role, authority-conferring acts (e.g., laying on of hands), and the power to determine appointee qualifications that began with the seven in Acts 6 was refined, not redefined, when Paul universalized the office of deacon in 1 Timothy 3:8-13. Below is a breakdown of those elements which include management structure, spiritual leaders, servant leader qualifications, authority to appoint, and formal ordination.

Management structure

It is clear the apostles were the spiritual leaders and overseers of the first church in Jerusalem. The apostles, therefore, had the authority to create the early church's management structure, which they discerned from the Holy Spirit. Acts 6 is the only place in Scripture where the apostles created an ordained group of servants that was ultimately formalized by the apostle Paul in 1 Timothy 3:8-13. Acts 6 and 1 Timothy 3 use the same flat management structure, with two tiers:

- **Tier one**: the spiritual leaders of the church. These leaders were the apostles initially and then the elders/pastors as seen across the whole of the New Testament.
- **Tier two**: servant-leaders managing tasks delegated by the spiritual leaders for the benefit of the church body.

There are no additional tiers of leadership or additional offices in the church. In Ephesians 4:11-12 Christ gave other gifted men to the church to equip the saints for the work of the ministry, but it is only the elders and deacons who function as the church's leaders.

Leadership Framework for Installing the Seven and Deacons

	Acts 6	1 Timothy 3
Management Structure	Two Tiers: Apostles & The Seven	Two Tiers: Elders & Deacons
Spiritual Leaders	Apostles	Elders
Servant Leaders	The Seven	Deacons
Qualifications	Acts 6: 3	1 Timothy 3:8-13
Appointing Authority	Apostles	Elders
Formal Ordination	Apostles	Elders

Figure 1

Headship

Acts 4 explains that the apostles had oversight over all things including the distribution of money and resources, as shown in verses 35-36: "owners of lands or houses sold them and brought the proceeds and it laid it at the apostles' feet and it was distributed to each as any had need." It was the apostles who determined when it was time to select men to serve, and, as we saw earlier in the chapter, they oversaw the entire process of serving. It is important to note the apostles were not abdicating their authority to the seven. They were not turning over the oversight of their office to the seven. The apostles delegated authority and responsibility to the seven to manage the assigned task.

Similarly, Paul established elders to be the spiritual leaders and exercise the same authority to oversee all elements of the church including the assigned tasks of the deacons. The apostles and the elders of 1 Timothy 3 both had the same headship: a plurality of men that were the spiritual leaders of the church who oversaw all its ministry-assisting servants/deacons. Now, it is certainly true that a young church can operate for a short period without deacons. The church in Acts operated for a while without the seven. However, a church cannot operate without elders. Paul instructs Titus to appoint elders in every city (Titus 1:5). He did not say to appoint deacons in every church. In the leadership structure established in 1 Timothy 3:1-13, the elders have headship and the deacons are complementary. As made clear above, it is the responsibility of the elders to determine the selection process, and to review and ordain deacons.

Servant-leaders

The seven of Acts 6 and deacons of 1 Timothy 3 are servant-leaders. Both are designed to serve the body of Christ. In Acts 6 the apostles were specific about the initial duties the seven were to apply in the church in Jerusalem. From Scripture we do not know if the duties for the seven were ever expanded or changed in any way. In 1 Timothy 3 Paul is not specific about the duties because it is for the elders of each church to establish those duties. As previously stated, a church needs elders to be properly established. A church does not initially need deacons to be established. Deacons come when the elders need to offload servant tasks so they can continue focus on the ministry of the Word and prayer (Acts 6:2). Deacons as formal leaders of the church have authority within the task(s) assigned them. They have the spiritual gift of service and an aspiration to be an official church officer. They manage those task(s) along with any other church members associated in those duties.

Qualifications

Formal biblical leadership structures begin with a framework of authority followed by qualifications and/or duties for their roles. God gave Adam and Eve the framework of authority for their roles, with the duties to multiply, subdue and have dominion over the earth (Gen 1:28; 2:20-24). Deuteronomy 33 provides the framework and role for Old Testament Priests. The Kings of Israel had God-given authority, roles and duties (Deut 17:14-17; 1 Sam 10:1; 1 Kgs 2:3-4). It follows that elders and deacons of Christ's church would expect to have a formal biblical leadership structure that provided a framework of authority with qualifications and duties. The qualification and duties of the seven were established in Acts 6:3 and for deacons in 1 Timothy 3:8-12.

A more detailed discussion of the deacon qualifications as given in 1 Timothy 3 appears in the next chapter. There are significant similarities of the listed qualifications for the seven and deacons. The qualifications for each passage are illustrated in the table below. In Acts 6 the apostles gave the community of believers three qualifications that each man was to possess:

Good Repute – a solid reputation, a man of character and admired conduct.[6]

Full of the Spirit – a man known to be led by the Spirit. A man that does not lean on his own understanding but prayerfully seeks the will of God in what he does. A man who walks by faith and not by sight.[7]

Full of Wisdom – a man who recognizes the difference between godly wisdom and man's wisdom. A man that when faced with decisions seeks God knowing that his own human mind can be a stumbling block and as such seeks godly wisdom in all things.[8]

The list of qualifications Paul provides in 1 Timothy 3 are not word-for-word identical. However, the essence of these qualities corresponds to the qualifications listed in Acts 6. In Figure 2, the qualifications set forth in both passages are compared.

Good repute is similar to dignified.[9] Both qualities are universal in nature and an observation made by others. They are qualities that inform the attitude and integrity of a man's conduct. A man who is full of the Spirit (living by God's wisdom) will not be double-tongued, will not have a problem

---

[6] Howard B. Foshee, *Now That You're a Deacon* (Nashville, TN: B&H Publishing Group, 1975), 43.
[7] Robert Naylor, *The Baptist Deacon* (Nashville, TN: Broadman and Holman Publishers, 1955), 17.
[8] J.D. O'Donnell, *Handbook for Deacons* (Nashville, TN: Randall House Publications, 1973), 23.
[9] "Good repute" is just one word—the present passive participle of *martureo*, which means, "to bear witness to." The same verb is used in Act 16:2c and 22:12 of a character "witness to" and approved by others. The English Bible translates it variously as "of honest report" (KJV), "of good reputation" (NASB), "who are known to be" (NIV), and "attested" (TNIV). See David G. Peterson, "First Timothy," in *The Pillar New Testament Commentary*, ed. D.A. Carson (Grand Rapids, MI: Eerdmans, 2009), 233.

with alcohol, will not be greedy, and will hold to the mystery of the faith. In short, he will be typified by the fruits of the Spirit listed in Galatians 5:22-23.

Qualifications of "The Seven" and Deacons

Acts 6:3	1 Timothy 3:8-9, 12
Good Repute	Dignified
Full of Spirit	Not Double-Tongued Not Addicted to Much Wine Not Greedy for Dishonest Gain Holds to the Mystery of the Faith
Full of Wisdom	Godly Wife Husband of One Wife Manages His Children and Household

Figure 2

A man full of godly wisdom will lean on God in all things of life including the choice and spiritual headship of a godly wife. He will be a one-woman man and will love and care for his wife while managing his children and household. Granted, this suggested grouping of the qualifications in Acts 6 and 1 Timothy 3 is a bit arbitrary. Any one of the 1 Timothy 3 qualifications may be better connected with a different qualification in Acts 6. The point is the exact grouping is not what is important, but clearly the qualities that Paul formally establishes for the office of deacon are in concert with those initiated by the apostles of Acts 6. The three qualities from Acts speak to a man's character, his being Spirit-led and being a man full of God's wisdom. Paul's list of qualities is more specific; however, they do complement the more general qualities of Acts 6.

Authority through appointing
As the spiritual-leaders and overseers of the first church in Jerusalem, the apostles had the authority to appoint and ordain the servants below them. The same is true with the elder structure established in 1 Timothy 3. Paul established the office of elder with the same authority. Elders are appointed by other elders (Titus 1:5), and elders appoint deacons. As we will see in the next chapter, elders can and should involve the community of believers in the appointment of elders and deacons. But, as discussed, the final responsibility for appointment of these servants rests on the elders.

Formal ordination
The New Testament model of praying with the laying of hands is a public ordinance showing the moving of the Holy Spirit— an act by which church leaders demonstrate to the community of believers how they have discerned the hand of God. In Acts 13 for example, Paul and Barnabas were sent on their missionary journey only after the church in Antioch fasted, prayed and laid hands on them (Acts 13:1-3). Further, in his first letter to Timothy, Paul encourages Timothy by reminding Timothy that the elders laid hands on him (1 Tim 4:14). Finally, a cornerstone scene in Acts is the apostles' laying hands on the seven (Acts 6:6). This biblical framework is faithfully applied in today's post-apostolic church in this way: after the final examination is complete and a church's spiritual leaders are convinced of God's hand moving to raise an elder or deacon, the elders should lay hands on the new leaders. The sole authority to do this lies with the elders of the church, as they

are the spiritual leaders and the ones responsible as undershepherds of Christ's church (Acts 20:28).

Overview of a Deacon's Ministry

Chapter six of this book is dedicated to addressing the details of a deacon's ministry. Here is a basic overview of the deacon's ministry, based on Acts 6 and 1 Timothy 3. The early chapters of Acts showed the apostles overseeing the ministry of the Word and managing all ministries and service areas of the church. It is assumed there are numerous servants helping the apostles at this stage, but it is clear from Acts 4:34-35 that the apostles did care for and manage activities in service of the poor.

In Acts 6, when the distribution to the widows grew out of control, the apostles assigned seven men to manage the problem. It is clear that the apostles oversaw the issue, determined the solution, and appointed the seven to the task. Scripture does not say if the seven were ever appointed other duties or if more servants were ordained and appointed to other tasks.

When Paul universalized the office of deacon in 1 Timothy 3:8-13, he established *service* as the scope of the diaconate ministry. According to the structure laid out by Paul, elders are the overseers, with ministry priority being to shepherd the flock of God (1 Pet 5:1-4). A church needs elders. A church cannot launch or operate without elders. And when functional service task(s) become too much for the elders to handle, just as happened with the apostles in Acts 6, then the elders are to appoint deacons to manage the needed task(s).

Paul did not specify tasks for deacons in 1 Timothy 3:8-13. By the Spirit he universalized a second office (deacons) that is under the direction and oversight of the first office (elders) with the simple ministry scope of service. Paul leaves it to the elders of every church to set the specific tasks for this second office, giving necessary flexibility and autonomy to each church in the execution thereof. Church elders today have the autonomy to focus their deacons on the areas of mercy as in Acts 6. Elders are also given the scriptural authority through 1 Timothy 3 to task deacons with anything the elders discern to be essential to the local body. This authority is missed by many today who are steeped in church tradition and fail to reckon with the fullness of Scripture on this topic.

Were the seven in Acts 6 deacons?
The debate as to whether the seven men in Acts 6 were the "first" deacons is asking the wrong question. When studying deacons, it is appropriate to study the Acts 6 passage because, as we have seen, the structure, qualifications, and tasks associated with this ministry mirror what Paul universalized in 1 Timothy 3:8-13. Christ, through the Holy Spirit, led the apostles in Acts 6 to initiate the formal appointment of servants that thirty years later Paul finalizes as the second office of deacon. In other words, Acts 6 initiated the serving office that Paul later universalized as deacons in 1 Timothy 3:8-13.

Because the universalized office of deacon was not established until approximately 63 AD by Paul, the seven appointed in Acts technically cannot be *titled* deacons. What is important to see, however, is that from the establishment of the church in Acts through three decades of growth thereafter, there is consistency in how the Holy Spirit guided the apostles in the structure and operations of the church. From Acts 6 to 1 Timothy 3 there is little, if any, change. Paul wrote 1 Timothy late in his ministry and universalized the office of elders and deacons under "the saying is trustworthy," which we will examine further in the next chapter. The key point is that Paul had been appointing leaders for many years, teaching leadership structure in the churches he planted. Paul's teaching on this subject was finally universalized in writing in 1 Timothy as prompted by the Holy Spirit, so that Christ's Bride—the Church—would have a biblical reference point for the leadership structure needed for proper headship and operation. Because the Church was a new entity (it did not exist in the Old Testament), a progressive and incremental transition of leadership structure was naturally necessary. This is the nature of progressive revelation.

First Timothy 3:1-13 thus is the New Testament model for church leadership structure, operations, examination and installation. Paul does not show any flexibility for modification in this passage. Churches are to have a simple leadership structure of elders (spiritual leaders) and deacons (servant leaders). The New Testament gives freedom to the local church to determine the appropriate number of elders and deacons for the specific needs, as long as there exists a plurality of elders (i.e., at least two). There also can be flexibility in how elders organize themselves for their shepherding and ministry-of-the-Word functions. Elders are to grow their leadership by appointing additional elders and deacons as needs arise, and as qualified men become available. In seeking and nurturing this growth, elders have tremendous freedom in involving the community of believers in the selection process of additional elders and deacons.

Paul clearly allows for local church autonomy within the structure he provides, but he gives no flexibility to add to or change the structure. Soon after Paul established this structure, however, post-apostolic-era generations changed both the leadership structure and operations of churches without proper authority. Today, it seems that many churches do not follow the structure of 1 Timothy 3 as laid out by Paul.

Summary of Acts 6 and 1 Timothy 3

The Holy Spirit moved Paul to formalize the offices of elder and deacon thirty years after the events of Acts 6. First Timothy 3:1-13 is the standard for leadership of Christ's church.

Acts 6:1-6 was Christ's first introduction to establish a unique set of servants being selected to serve his Church. The first church in Jerusalem was just getting established. The apostles (the spiritual shepherds of the church) were operating as the elders of that church. The church was growing rapidly (Acts 2:41) as many Jews were coming to faith, even many of the Jewish priests (Acts 6:7). Though the title of "deacon" is not established in this passage, it is clear the apostles determined a need for, and selected, leaders to serve and manage the issue of food distribution to the widows. The apostles needed to keep focus on the ministry of the Word within the growing church, so they empowered the community of believers to select men to handle the important issue with the widows. This leadership structure established by Christ through the apostles in Acts was later universalized by the apostle Paul in 1 Timothy 3:8-13.

Paul refined the deacon-selection process by delineating deacon qualifications and detailing how the two offices—elders and deacons—functioned together. This process will be further explored in the coming chapters.

There is debate today as to whether the men of Acts 6:1-6 should be considered deacons. As we've seen, Acts 6 and 1 Timothy 3 mirror each other in describing the qualifications, structure, and role of deacons. The debate of whether the men in Acts 6 were deacons distracts from the important issue of how consistent the model was for selecting servants/deacons over the thirty-year period from the days of the early church to the time of Paul's letter to Timothy. We should therefore conclude that the office of deacon was *initiated* (not in its final form) with the seven servants the apostles appointed in Acts 6 then universalized by Paul in 1 Timothy 3.[10] Even the church office of elder was reconstituted with the birth of the Church during the New Covenant era. Elders existed during the Mosaic economy and during the ministry of Jesus but their role and qualifications were recalibrated by the apostles in keeping with being shepherds of the body of Christ, the Church. So Paul finalizes and universalizes the qualifications for both the office and deacon and elder in 1 Timothy 3.

Technically you can't call the men in Acts 6 deacons simply because the office had not been formalized by name yet. Acts 6 uses the verb form of *daikoneo* but not the noun. The noun as a title was used by Paul in 1 Timothy 3. At the same time our study has revealed all the similarities between Acts 6 and 1 Timothy 3. As the Jerusalem church grew, the apostles appointed the servants in Acts 6 and later appointed elders. Both the elder and deacon offices were universalized by Paul in 1 Timothy 3 and Titus 1. The headship of the church started with apostles and transitioned to elders. The office of deacon was initiated with the seven in Acts 6 and formalized in 1 Timothy 3.

There are several important developments that did come out of Acts 6 that have had a positive influence in the church over the last 2,000 years its history.

---

[10] Ralph Earle, *The Expositor's Bible Commentary: 1, 2 Timothy, Vol 11*, ed., Frank E. Gaebelein (Grand Rapids, MI: Zondervan Publishing House, 1976), 367.

1. *Representative government.* The church body was involved in the selection of their leaders. Throughout the Old Testament leaders were primarily appointed by God and seldom were the people involved in the approval or selection process. Representative government was initiated in Acts 6 and remains an important and necessary part of Christ's church. The church body needs to know and be a part of the selection process of its leaders.

2. *Delegation of authority and responsibility.* The apostles ordained seven men as servants, giving them both authority and responsibility to handle tasks (e.g., service to widows) in place of the apostles, on behalf of Christ for the apostles, and for the benefit of the greater body.

3. *Active management.* There were already servants helping the widows in Acts 6 prior to ordaining the seven, but the Hellenistic widows were not being treated fairly. The apostles needed active managers. Part of the seven's role was to manage other servants in the church for the church's benefit.

When discussing the roles, qualifications, selection process, and other topics relating to deacons, Acts 6 and 1 Timothy 3 are foundational. Though the men of Acts 6 were not deacons, they initiated what later became the office of deacon as described in 1 Timothy 3. So, Acts 6 remains a major reference point when studying the topic of deacons. The two passages are interlaced. However, 1 Timothy 3 is the primary text because it describes when the office was universalized.

The legacy of Acts 6 includes servants being affirmed/selected by the church body, working under the delegated authority of the elders, serving the church directly, and helping to manage other church servants on behalf of the elders, all for the spiritual and temporal blessing of the church body.

"And let them also **be tested first; then let them serve** as deacons **if they prove themselves blameless.**"
1 Timothy 3:10

5

The Selection Process and Qualifications

The interpretation of 1 Timothy 3:10 poses challenges. Some say verse 10 is only about examining a potential deacon, stressing the call for the elders and church body to examine the character and past service of the man that is being considered for the office. Others hold that verse 10 is both a call for examination as well as one of the listed qualifications that must be addressed and approved by the church to install a deacon. Others still make strong distinctions, saying that verse 10 has two separate qualifications: to be proved through testing; to be blameless, meaning there is no wrong charge that can be brought against a prospective deacon.[1] In this verse, "blameless" is not associated with the "testing" earlier in the verse. "Testing" is viewed as standing on its own similar to being dignified, or of good reputation.

---

[1] Robert Naylor, *The Baptist Deacon* (Nashville, TN: Broadman and Holman Publishers, 1955), 28-30;"the central idea of the word 'proved' is that of testing or the demonstration of the individual's capacity." "[Blameless] means that no charge of wrongdoing has been leveled against a man or could be brought." Authors of this view see examining the deacon candidate as v. 10a, "These men must also first be tested," as one qualification, and v. 10, "if blameless" as a separate qualification as being above reproach.

The grammatical structure and context of verse 10 determines it to be both a call to examine a deacon candidate, "let them be tested," and a qualification that must be concluded from the testing "found to be blameless." The candidate is to be fully examined by the church and found to be fully qualified across all qualifications, "blameless." "Blameless" is not a stand-alone qualification separate from testing/examination.

Furthermore, 3:10 in whole reveals a *selection process* —being properly tested and installed as a deacon is not simply checking the box of character qualifications followed up with an email to say "you're in." It is a process that involves examination by the entirety of the church, the candidate, the elders and the church body, followed by a formal appointment and ordination as a servant-leader of the church, "then let them serve as deacons."

In this chapter, we will first look at the selection process and the autonomy of the local church elders in this process. Next, we will look at contextual issues of 1 Timothy 3:8-13, and then an explication of deacon qualifications.

Identify Candidates

Paul does not dictate how a deacon candidate should be initially recognized. This leaves it open for elders of each church to make a determination for themselves how the candidate should be identified, with flexibility to change over time as determined by a church's elders. Paul also does not provide the details on how to determine if a man meets the qualifications of 1 Timothy 3:8-13, nor does he dictate what kinds of service a potential deacon should have performed in the past. Paul does not dictate when and how the community of believers should be a part of the process. Neither does he provide a list the duties of deacons, other than saying they are to serve.[2] In short, Paul does not give specifics on several things, allowing the elders to make determinations as they see fit. But Paul is specific that deacons are "servants," not "ministers of the Word." What is clear is that, while the elders oversee the process and make the ultimate choice on a deacon candidate, the manner in which a community of believers is involved can be determined by the elders.

Elders are the ones to oversee the process. Just as in Acts 6, the apostles affirm the deacon's qualifications, examine the candidate, and lay hands on each man, appointing him to service. The church is also to be involved as it was in Acts 6. There the apostles had the community choose the seven men for them to examine and approve. Acts 6 established the involvement of the church in the selection of its leadership. This chapter illustrates the importance of representative church leaders. Church leadership is not to be autocratic and dictatorial. The community of believers needs to be involved in the selection process even though the ultimate authority rests with the elders.

Just *how* the community of believers is involved, however, is a decision for the elders. Many churches today, for example, assert that Acts 6 posits a pure democracy wherein the community of believers selected the seven independently of any elder oversight. Some churches even argue the elders are not to be involved at all in the selection process.[3] Others suggest it is the responsibility for the body to elect its leaders

---

[2] In the New Testament there is only one thing deacons are commanded to do: serve! The only imperative for deacons in 1 Timothy 3 is *diakoneitosan,* which means, "let them serve" (v. 10). This is God's genius. There are endless ways to "serve" in meeting the practical needs of the local church. This sole command also allows for limitless flexibility in the role of deacon to meet the ever-changing demands of the dynamic Body of Christ.

[3] Harold Nichols, *The Work of the Deacon & Deaconess* (Valley Forge, PA: Judson Press, 2014), 34.

(elders and deacons) and then it's the elders' duty to appoint them publicly.[4] Acts 6 does set a baseline standard wherein the body is to be involved in the selection of its leaders. However, 1 Timothy 3:10 formalizes the process granting the elders flexibility to determine just how the body is affirm its leaders. So, the elders have the autonomy to determine how the church body is to be involved in the selection process. Chapter nine discusses best practices addressing a variety of practical elements related to deacons. One of those elements is how to involve the church body when selecting deacons.

Selection Process

The selection process in Acts 6 and 1 Timothy 3 are virtually identical; the difference comes in the implementation. In Acts 6, the apostles presented the qualifications to the community of believers, and then delegated to the community the initial selection of the seven men. Following completion of this step, the apostles examined the seven (set before them v. 6) and then appointed them to the task with formal ordination. The apostles in Acts 6 were very precise on how and when the community would be involved. Thirty years later when the apostle Paul is giving written instructions to formalize the office of deacon in 1 Timothy 3, he did not prescribe how the congregation was to be involved in the selection process. Rather, he gave the local church elders freedom to determine the process. The verb "tested" is in the imperative form meaning it is not optional or cursory. The testing is obligatory, serious, and thorough, and should involve the entire church.

First Timothy 3:10 provides the textual source for the selection process. It is elegantly simple and straightforward.

---

[4] Benjamin Merkle, *40 Questions About Elders and Deacons* (Grand Rapids, MI: Kregel Publications, 2008), 47. This view is also supported by Millard J. Erickson, *Christian Theology*, 2nd ed. (Grand Rapids, MI: Baker, 1988), 1092.

The Selection Process and Qualifications

First examine the deacon candidate. *"Let them be tested first."* If the examination shows that the candidate meets all qualifications appropriately—*"if they prove themselves blameless"*—then the church has found a qualified deacon and should ordain him into office—*"then let him serve."* The selection process has four steps.

1. *Examine a candidate's qualifications.* A candidate's previous church service should be lengthy enough to fully examine him in light of the listed qualifications in verses 8-12, verifying the required qualities are evident in his life. This "testing" is from a review of the candidate's past service. It does not mean a candidate should be given a task to accomplish and then be evaluated. In Acts 6, the congregation in Jerusalem looked at the qualifications for the seven men through the lens of the past. The examination of a deacon candidate begins by looking at their current and past service in the church, weighing it through the grid of the qualifications set forth in verses 8-12. The implication is that a comprehensive examination includes the entire church body. The elders have autonomy to choose how to include the body in the process, and the freedom to change that process as they see fit. That does not allow the elders to manipulate or authoritatively assert their will. Rather, as the needs of the church change over time the process can be changed.

2. *Examine the candidate's service alongside the elders.* In Acts 6, the apostles appointed the seven so they

could continue in the ministry of the Word while the seven ministered to the widows. The men they appointed needed to be more than good servants. They needed spiritual qualifications. They needed to be men whose service was to be done in excellence as unto the Lord. As servants, their quality, timeliness, effectiveness, and excellence were essential. Deacons need to understand their tasks are delegated to them by God through the elders. "A *diakonos* in the ordinary sense was one who executed the commands of another, a servant, an attendant, a minister."[5] They need to have the demeanor and ability to work alongside the elders in their service. When examining a candidate's past service, assessing how he has worked alongside elders is essential.

3. *Examine a candidate's attitude and how he works with others.* Is the candidate shown to be blameless? In other words, in his tenure of service, has he shown himself to be faithful across all the qualifications? His character and giftedness should be evident as well as his ability to coordinate with and manage the other church servants. He needs to show a proper demeanor and forthrightness when working and communicating with other church servants. He needs to exhibit proper conduct and flexibility in

---

[5] Homer A. Kent, Jr., *The Pastoral Epistles* (Winona Lake, IN: BMH Books, 1995), 132.

accepting delegated tasks when working with elders.

4. *"Let them serve."* If a man's service to his church has demonstrated he possesses the necessary qualifications—that he has worked well with the elders and the other church servants—and if through this examination the man has proven to be blameless, then it is time to affirm his qualifications with the body and the elders and to ordain him into formal service.

Christ's selection process, given to Paul through the Holy Spirit, is simple and straightforward, and it gives local elders freedom within the process.

In summary, a deacon candidate's God-given talents and giftedness to serve, along with their attitudes, desires and willingness to serve, will be clearly manifested. When the elders have determined that a potential deacon meets the qualifications—that he works well with the elders and church members, that his past service shows him to be blameless and has been affirmed by the members—the church body has found a deacon.

Other Contextual Considerations in 1 Timothy 3

There are three exegetical observations that help us properly interpret 1 Timothy 3:8-13. The first involves a discussion of the of the phrase "likewise" (v. 8). The second are the two conjunctions "and" and "also" used in 3:10. The third considers the phrase, "the saying is trustworthy" (v. 1).

Likewise
There are several places in the New Testament in which

"likewise" is used as a literary device: it is an adverb that links to a premise stated earlier in the context. It implies a parallel. "Likewise," (*hosautos*) means "in the same way" or "after the same manner." Below is an example from earlier in 1 Timothy:

> [8]Therefore I want the men in every place to pray, lifting up holy hands, without anger and dispute. [9]Likewise, *I want* women to adorn themselves with proper clothing, modestly and discreetly, not with braided hair and gold or pearls or expensive apparel (2:8-9, NASB).

The "likewise" in v. 9 links back to "I want" in v. 8. Paul desires certain things for men and other things for women. The word for "I want" used in v. 8 is not present in the Greek in v. 9. However, like the NASB quoted above, some English translations insert the words of the premise ("I want") after "likewise" in v. 9. This is a legitimate insertion because, while the word is not actually in the original, it is nevertheless understood to be a part of the sentence.

The use of "likewise" also indicates that the passage is one unit of thought. In 1 Timothy 2:8:9, Paul is writing about conduct in worship and addressing his expectations of both men and women.

We now turn back to 1 Timothy 3:1-13 and review the "likewise" statement:

> [1] The saying is trustworthy: If any man aspires to the office of overseer, he desires a noble task.[2] Therefore an overseer **must be** above reproach, the husband of one wife, sober-minded, self-controlled, respectable, hospitable, able to teach,[3] not a drunkard, not violent but gentle, not quarrelsome, not a lover of money.

⁴He must manage his own household well, with all dignity keeping his children submissive, ⁵for if someone does not know how to manage his own household, how will he care for God's church. ⁶He must not be a recent convert, or he may become puffed up with conceit and fall into the condemnation of the devil. ⁷Moreover, he must be well thought of by outsiders, so that he may not fall into disgrace, into a snare of the devil.

⁸deacons likewise *must be* dignified, not double-tongued, not addicted to much wine, not greedy for dishonest gain. ⁹They must hold the mystery of the faith with a clear conscience. ¹⁰And let them also be tested first; then let them serve as deacons if they prove themselves blameless. ¹¹Their wives likewise *must be* dignified, not slanderers, but sober-minded, faithful in all things. ¹²Let deacons each be the husband of one wife, managing their children and their own households well. ¹³For those who have served well as deacons obtain for themselves a high standing and great confidence in the faith that is in Christ Jesus.

The term likewise in v. 8 and v. 11 link back to v. 2 **"must be."**[6] Elders **must** have the characteristics listed in vv. 1-7. Deacons **must** have the characteristics laid out in vv. 8-12. And their wives **must** have the characteristics set forth in v. 11.

---

[6] John MacArthur and Richard Mayhue, *Biblical Doctrine: A Systematic Summary of Bible Truth* (Wheaton, IL: Crossway, 2017), 771.

The term likewise in v. 8 and v. 11 also identifies that the passage of vv. 1-13 is one unit of thought. In this case, Paul's instruction on church leadership is clearly delineated in these verses, and the verses before 3:1 and after 3:13 address other topics.

And…also
First Timothy 3:10 starts with the conjunction *kai* (and) followed with a second conjunction *de* (also). "**And** let them **also** be tested first." Some authors see the double conjunction requiring deacons to be tested just as elders are to be tested. Connecting the two offices in the seriousness, comprehensiveness and fullness of their testing. The word "and" is all that is needed to connect deacons to testing. The second conjunction is an unnecessary word "also" unless it is relating the testing of deacons to the testing elders. Other scholars believe the double conjunction is to strengthen the imperative of testing first before installing a deacon. The former explanation ties the two offices together both as the only offices of the church and the seriousness of examination within their roles.[7]

The saying is trustworthy
The phrase "the saying is trustworthy" is unique to Paul's pastoral epistles in Timothy and Titus, appearing a total of five times and each time introducing a basic truth of great importance—a truth that was likely familiar to the believers in the churches Paul had planted. These trustworthy sayings are self-evident truths, axioms that become creeds about different areas of doctrine. One of the sayings is about leadership—the call to ministry—and the other four sayings are elements of

---

[7] Alexander Strauch, *Paul's Vision for the Deacons* (Littleton, CO: Lewis and Roth Publishers, 2017), 107.

Christian beliefs.[8] Below is the location of each trustworthy saying and a summary of the topic:

> "**The saying is trustworthy** and deserving of full acceptance, that Christ Jesus came into the world to save sinners..." (1 Tim 1:15).
>
> "**The saying is trustworthy**: If anyone aspires to the office of overseer, he desires a noble task" (1 Tim 3:1).
>
> "for while bodily training is of some value, godliness is of value in every way, as it holds promise for the present life and also for the life to come. **The** *[previous]* **saying is trustworthy** and deserving of full acceptance" (1 Tim 4:8-9).
>
> "**The saying is trustworthy**, If we have died with him, we will also live with him; if we endure, we will also reign with him; if we deny him, he also will deny us; if we are faithless, he remains faithful..." (2 Tim 2:11).
>
> "**The saying is trustworthy [in vv. 4-7]**, and I want you to insist on these things, so that those who have believed in God may be careful to devote themselves to good works. These things are excellent and profitable for people" (Titus 3:8).

Turning specifically to the trustworthy statement in 1 Timothy 3:1: "The saying is trustworthy: If anyone aspires to the office of overseer, he desires a noble task." The fact that a man

---

[8]. John MacArthur, *The MacArthur New Testament Commentary: 1 Timothy* (Chicago, IL: Moody Publishers, 1995), 92-93.

aspires to become an elder is an important qualification. It is a qualification that many authors neglect to independently identify when writing on subject of elders and deacons. It is a qualification many churches miss in their evaluation of a candidate. God's call for a man to become an under-shepherd of Christ in the leadership of his local church is daunting. It is the call placed into the heart of a man that is beyond the gifts of teaching or service. Part of determining the qualifications of an elder candidate is determining if and why he aspires to the office.

Therefore, when addressing the qualifications of a deacon, "aspiration" should be considered. At a high-level, Paul is outlining proper church leadership structure across the context of 1 Timothy 3:1-13. The term "likewise" links the office of deacon to the office of elder, and the "trustworthy" statement identifies the importance of proper motivation in a leader. The combination of the passage context, plus the "trustworthy" statements, implies the qualification of proper aspiration to the office of deacon. Elders and deacons make up the church's leadership structure, and both must have the proper aspiration for the office or their pursuit of leadership is illegitimate. Sadly, the testimony of church history is that far too many men "desire" church leadership and authority for wrong reasons. Aspiration is a qualification for both elders and deacons, and it needs to be a part of the evaluation of leadership candidates. Many authors suggest the motivation and character of potential deacon candidates as part of the examination in 1 Timothy 3:10. This is discussed further in the aspiration qualification below.

Qualifications

Interestingly enough, after 2,000 years of church history Bible scholars, pastors and authors do not agree on deacon qualifications. I have found authors with as few as eight qualifications and as many as sixteen.[9] There are groupings along the lines of biblical interpretation and systematic views of Scripture. Many with strong congregational views include the three qualifications for the seven in Acts 6 as part of deacon qualifications while others do not.[10] It is also common for congregationalist to interpret the description of Stephen in Acts 6:5 (a man full of faith) as a qualification for deacons.[11] These same people will commonly interpret the promise of Christ in 1 Timothy 3:13 to be a qualification for deacons.[12]

For those who believe 1 Timothy 3:11 are wives of male deacons, v. 11 is then a qualification for a deacon. For those who view v. 11 as creating the role of deaconesses, female assistants, or women deacons, then v. 11 include qualifications for these female roles are not associated with male deacons. Then there is at least one author who simply ignores v.11 choosing not to state a position.[13]

Thabiti Anyabwile does not list deacons managing their children and household in 1 Timothy 3:12 as a qualification.[14] Then there are those who add arbitrary qualifications not in the Bible based on church tradition and preferences. Naylor

---

[9] Ralph Earle, *The Expositor's Bible Commentary: 1, 2 Timothy, Vol. 11*, ed., Frank E. Gaebelein (Grand Rapids, MI: Zondervan Publishing House, 1976), 366-368; Naylor, *The Baptist Deacon*, 21-31.
[10] Henry Webb, *Deacons: Servant Models in the Church* (Nashville, TN: B&H Publishing Group, 2001), 13.
[11] J.D. O'Donnell, *Handbook for Deacons* (Nashville, TN: Randall House Publications, 1973), 22.
[12] Howard B. Foshee, *Now That You're a Deacon* (Nashville, TN: B&H Publishing Group, 1975), 44.
[13] Thabiti M. Anyabwile, *Finding Faithful Elders and Deacons* (Wheaton, IL: Crossway, 2012), 19-43.
[14] Ibid.

believes deacons need to be businessmen, "deacons should have certain secular qualifications" based on the KJV translation of Acts 6:3: "Wherefore, brethren, look ye out among you seven men of honest report, full of the Holy Ghost and wisdom, whom we may appoint over **this business**." Naylor concludes, "it is safe to say that these seven were business-men…it is good to select men of practical business judgement and experience as deacons."[15] Nichols suggests churches can have other deacon qualifications outside of 1 Timothy 3:8-13 that are "rooted" in history, culture, tradition, church polity or other chosen passages of Scripture.[16]

Across the spectrum of authorship, the only fully agreed qualifications are the five listed in vv. 8-9. The vast majority of authors also agree with the two (husband of one wife, managing children and household well) listed in v. 12.

Three of the major areas of disagreement among commentators are around whether to include the qualifications of Acts 6:3 and the interpretation of 1 Timothy 3:10 and verse 11. Additionally, I hold that aspiring to the office of deacon is a qualification based on the grammatical and contextual elements previously discussed is this chapter. Many authors agree a deacon needs to have proper aspirations to leadership, however, they do not list is as an independent qualification but rather it should be part of the examination of 1 Timothy 3:10.

---

[15] Naylor, *The Baptist Deacon*, 20-21. Naylor has the longest list of qualifications including the extra-biblical requirement of being a businessman based on the KJV translation of *chreia* as business. *Chreia* is much better translated as "task," "responsibility" or "duty" as is seen in the ESV, NIV, NASB, CSB. "[T]he instruction in the selection of the seven was that they should be men who could be appointed 'over this business.' It is very plain that the new rank of ministerial orders was not being created but that secular responsibilities were be distributed. If too much is not made of the modern meaning of the term, it is safe to say these seven were businessmen. The word 'business' should be discussed a little to prevent any misunderstanding. The Greek word is *chreia* and basically means 'need.' It is so translated twenty-five times. This is the only place that it is translated 'business' (KJV and others).… It is good to select men of practice business judgement and experience as deacons."
[16] Nichols, *The Work of the Deacon*, 26.

The Selection Process and Qualifications

	Qualifications of Deacons by Author												
	Anyabwile	Foshee	Naylor	O'Donnell	Webb	Van Dam	Getz	McArthur	Nichols	Earle	Strauch	Merkle	Geisler	Douglas
Acts 6														
Good Repute v.3	X	X	X	X	X	X								
Full of the Spirit v.3	X	X	X	X	X	X								
Full of wisdom v.3	X	X	X	X	X	X								
1 Tim 3														
Aspire v.1														X
Dignified v.8	X	X	X	X	X	X	X	X	X	X	X	X	X	X
Not insincere v.8	X	X	X	X	X	X	X	X	X	X	X	X	X	X
Not much wine v.8	X	X	X	X	X	X	X	X	X	X	X	X	X	X
Not greedy v.8	X	X	X	X	X	X	X	X	X	X	X	X	X	X
Hold to faith v.9	X	X	X	X	X	X	X	X	X	X	X	X	X	X
Tested & blameless v.10	X			X	X	X	X	X	X	X		X	X	X
Wife of deacon v.11		X	X	X	X	X				X	X	X	X	
Husband one wife v.12		X	X	X	X	X	X	X	X	X	X	X	X	X
Children & home v.12		X	X	X	X	X	X	X	X	X	X	X	X	X
Unusual Views														
Tested v.10		X	X											
Blameless v.10		X	X											
Bold in faith v.13		X	X		X									
Full of faith- Acts 6:5		X	X	X	X									
Extra-biblical														
Business man			X					X						
Total Qualifications	9	15	16	13	14	12	8	8	9	8	8	9	9	10

Sifting through the confusion, I hold that there are ten qualifications for deacons all based on the Apostle Paul's list in 1 Timothy 3:1-13. Following is a brief overview.

1. *Aspiration*

As introduced in the previous section, the first qualification for a deacon is that he is to aspire to the office. This is a critical qualification and one that is overlooked by many. A man must have the proper, God-given desire to become a deacon—a call to formal leadership in the church beyond the mere desire to serve. God himself raises up the man for the role by giving him the spiritual gift of service (cf. 1 Cor 12:28; Rom 12:7), granting him the character qualifications necessary to fulfill it, and proper desire for the role as a church leader. He is affirmed by the congregation then ordained by the elders and looked to by the congregation as a leader and role model.[17] This desire and formal recognition by the elders is unlike what other faithful church members experience. And, as with elders, no one should be elevated to leadership unless God has placed the proper desire in his heart. Most authors do not list aspiration as an independent qualification for the office of deacon. However, many suggest the examination process of 1 Timothy 3:10 includes evaluating a prospective deacon's motivations, character, and heart.

> Merkle's discussion of deacon examination includes the *heart* of a deacon in his service. "Although Paul does not specify what type of testing is to take place at minimum, the candidate's personal background, reputation, and theological positions should be examined. But not only should the moral, spiritual, and doctrinal aspects be tested; the congregation also must consider the person's actual services in the church. A person with a deacon's *heart* is one who looks for opportunities to serve."[18]

> Nichols in his discussion of deacon examination believes their *heart* and actions are to be that of Christ and visible to those of the congregation. "[D]eacons should try to live as an example of 'the new person in Jesus Christ.' This is not to impose an expectation of perfection on the prospect or active deacon, but it is

---

[17] John M. Frame, *Systematic Theology: An Introduction to Christian Belief* (Phillipsburg, NJ: P&R Publishing, 2013), 682. "Learning by imitation is an important means of sanctification, a vital means of appropriating the Word of God...we should ourselves seek to be examples that can be imitated by our fellow believers."

[18] Merkle, *40 Questions*, 235-236.

to acknowledge that a spiritual leaders must indeed lead where he or she invites others to follow."[19]

Naylor in his discussion of v. 10 suggests a part of testing a deacon includes examining his *motivation* through Galatians 6:4. "In Galatians 6:4, the instruction is to 'let every man prove his own work.' All of Christianity is subject to testing. Jesus invited everyone that heard him to weigh that which he said, to test it in his own heart and experience and reach a decision on that basis. If that is the principle on which the kingdom of God is built, it certainly is the principle by which God intend that men be selected for places of leadership in the churches."[20]

Strauch in his discussion of v. 10 applies the standard for elders in 1 Timothy 5:22, 24-25 to deacons when evaluating the fullness of their character which includes the *proper aspiration* to the office of elder. Strauch, after referencing the passage, states, "Paul is referring here to the appointment of an elder to office, but the same principle applies equally to the office of deacon. No one should be appointed to office if the church has not first invested the time and effort to properly examine the candidate's character and credentials."[21]

Whether you agree that aspiration is its own qualification, or if you view that it falls under 3:10's examination is not important, the point is this: part of evaluating a deacon candidate is to

---

[19] Nichols, *The Work of the Deacon*, 16.
[20] Naylor, *The Baptist Deacon*, 28-29.
[21] Strauch, *Paul's Vision*, 114-115.

specifically address their motivations and heart. This evaluation is necessary to avoid two potential issues. The first is ordaining a man who has an inappropriate view of being a servant-leader --either being overly authoritarian and asserting their own will, or overly meek with an improper view of serving and leading. The second potential issue is finding a man who meets all other qualifications is a good servant but has no desire to be an official church leader. This man may potentially accept the position because the church has a need and he feels obligated to serve, but he has no true passion to do so.

Over the years I have met men that were solid leaders in life and vocation and meet the other qualifications listed in vv. 8-12 but who did not aspire to become a deacon. Being a servant and being a servant-leader is not the same. If a man does not *aspire* to the position, we must assume that God has not called him to church leadership. He therefore should not be pressured into the position. A deacon has the spiritual gift of service and a calling to hold the office of a church leader.

The only thing worse than a void in leadership is installing a poor leader or unmotivated leader. Aspiration to the office of deacon is an essential heart issue, not easily seen as many of the other qualifications. Determining if a deacon candidate has the proper aspiration is essential. It is the first question I have for a deacon prospect.

2. *Worthy of respect/dignified*

This qualification pertains to the moral character and reputation of a deacon. These are critical in church leaders, whose conduct is seen by people inside and outside the church.[22] This is the first of the character qualities because it ties into the others that follow in the verses. A man who is

---

[22] Strauch, *Paul's Vision*, 89-90.

properly worthy of respect is not double-minded, addicted to wine, greedy, or unfaithful to his wife. These qualifications are very similar to the qualification given by the apostles for selecting the seven in Acts 6:3—to be "of good repute." "Worthy of respect" is a characteristic of Christ; he never shaded the truth, misled, or flattered others.[23] Christ is the model, always sincere in how he addressed and how he worked with others, whether a Pharisee or beggar.

3. Not double-tongued

To be double-tongued is to say one thing and mean another, or to habitually say one thing to one person and something different to another.[24] Whereas a double-tongued man undermines his credibility, a man of truthful speech creates a foundation of trust and good working relationships with the body and other leaders.[25] The root of being double-tongued is either being double-minded, which James 1:8 tells us leads to spiritual instability, or it comes from a sinful desire to conceal truth, leading to lying or deceit. The word of a deacon carries the weight of church leadership; it reflects back on the elders who ordained him, so the deacon must always be forthright and honest.

4. Not addicted to much wine

Deacons are to be sober and self-controlled; anything less is a negative reflection on the reputation of the deacon and the church.[26] This is not a ban on wine. Wine is used throughout the Bible; Jesus' first miracle was making water into wine (John 2:9). During the Last Supper, Jesus passed the cup of wine

---

[23] Anyabwile, *Finding Faithful*, 28.
[24] I.H. Marshall and Philip H. Towner, *The Pastoral Epistles* (London: T&T Clark, 2004), 489.
[25] Strauch, *Paul's Vision*, 92-93.
[26] Cornelis Van Dam, *The Deacon: Biblical Foundations for Today's Ministry of Mercy* (Grand Rapids, MI: Reformation Heritage Books, 2016), 65.

(Luke 22:9). Paul tells Timothy to take some wine for his stomach (1 Tim 5:23). This prohibition, therefore, is a prohibition on the *excessive use* of wine. A deacon should not be addicted to wine and should never be intoxicated. He is to be controlled by the Spirit (Eph 5:18), not by alcohol or his passions (Gal 5:16-24). [27] Proverbs 20:1 and 23:29-35 explain that one under the influence of alcohol is not wise and has many related issues and problems in life. A lack of self-control with alcohol is not godly and considered debauchery in Scripture.

5. Not greedy for dishonest gain
A deacon is not to seek out gain in a dishonorable way or at the expense of others. In Jesus' time, the scribes would financially devastate widows: "Beware of the scribes, who like to walk around in long robes, and love personal greetings in the marketplaces, and chief seats in the synagogues and places of honor at banquets, who devour widows' houses, and for appearance's sake offer long prayers. These will receive all the more condemnation" (Luke 20:46-47). False teachers and men of the world have evil desires for money and pursue dishonest gain (Titus 1:11; 1 Tim 6:3-10).[28] Deacons need to be free from a love of money that could compromise their attitude and actions.

6. Must hold to the mystery of the faith with a clear conscience
The mystery of the faith is the salvation believers have in Christ, which includes the fullness of the gospel, the person of Christ, and the Holy Spirit who indwells believers. However, it is not enough merely to believe these truths; deacons must also live them. Every deacon should strive to live according to the

---

[27] Strauch, *Paul's Vision*, 94.
[28] Van Dam, *The Deacon*, 65.

pattern prescribed in 2 Corinthians 1:12: "For our boast is this, the testimony of our conscience, that we behaved in the world with simplicity and godly sincerity, not by earthly wisdom but by the grace of God, and supremely so toward you." Deacons are not required to teach, but they must live lives that show their maturity as believers to the church. Deacons must be solid in their faith.

7. *Tested first*

Verse 10 has three phrases and English translations handle them differently. The NIV, CSB and others directly connect the "being blameless" phrase with the testing, structuring the sentence contextually. The ESV, NASV, KJV and others hold to the Greek grammatical sentence structure, leaving the "being blameless" phrase after "let them serve." Below is the Greek followed by several English translations:

καὶ	οὗτοι	δὲ	δοκιμαζέσθωσαν	πρῶτον,
[and]	[these]	[also]	[let them be tested]	[first]

εἶτα	διακονείτωσαν	ἀνέγκλητοι	ὄντες
[then]	[let them serve]	[blameless]	[being]

NIV – They must first be tested; and then **if there is nothing against them**, let them serve as deacons.

CSB – They must also be tested first; **if they prove blameless**, then they can serve as deacons.

ESV – And let them also be tested first; then let them serve as deacons **if they prove themselves blameless**.

KJV – And let these also first be proved; then let them use the office of a deacon, **being found blameless**.

NASB – These men must also first be tested; then have them serve as deacons **if they are beyond reproach**.

As discussed earlier in the chapter the testing is properly connected to being blameless. The testing is to involve the entire church body. It is a call for the deacon candidate to examine his heart and reflect on the character qualifications. To affirm his spiritual giftedness includes service (1Cor 12:4-6) and God's call to the position of leadership. It is a call for the elders to examine all qualifications and the deacons prior/current service and how the candidate interacts with the elders. The elders are to establish how the body is to be involved in the examination and affirmation of a deacon candidate. It is a call for the church body to examine the candidate and respond back to the elders.

Verse ten is a qualification; the candidate must meet all qualifications and is to be considered blameless. Verse 10 also lays out the selection process as previously discussed.

8. Their wives

There is much debate on whether 3:11 is providing the qualifications of deacons' "wives" or if it is addressing qualifications of women deacons, deaconesses, or women that work with deacons/elders. The first word of v. 11 in Greek is "women." There is no word for "wife" in Greek. The context of a given passage determines if the meaning is "woman" or "wife" and thus translated accordingly into English. Chapter eight is dedicated to this debate. Paul gives four qualifications in v. 11 for the women:

> "Dignified" – The term "likewise" used in v. 8 is used again here to say that the women must be dignified. This is the same qualification as above; here it is applied to the women's moral character and reputation.
>
> "Not Slanderers" – The Greek word used here is *diabolous*, the same root word used for "devil." More than the common definition of slander—verbally telling an untruth about someone—*diabolous* refers to all wrongful speech, lies, false rumors, malicious gossip, innuendos, and deceit meant to damage the reputation or be injurious to another.[29] These verbal outcomes come from root issues of anger, jealousy, bitterness, or other sinful attitudes that lead to inappropriate speech.
>
> "Sober-Minded" – This is the same word used for elders in v. 2, meaning "clear in thinking," "not overly swayed by emotion," and "able to reason through dynamic or difficult issues."
>
> "Faithful in All Things" – Faithfulness in all endeavors is a goal for all believers (Gal 5:22; Matt 25:21). It is from this that Paul calls for faithfulness in the women. Whether this passage is translated as deacons' wives, women deacons, or deaconesses,

---

[29] Strauch, *Paul's Vision*, 125.

Paul requires these women to be Christ-centered servants and faithful in all they do.

These women are to be serious Christian women that do not engage in inappropriate activities. They are to be clear-minded and level-headed in their thinking and faithful in their interactions and activities.

9. *Husband of one wife*

The meaning of this phrase is highly debated. Broadly speaking, interpreters fall into one of two camps. Those that view husband of one wife through the lens of marital status and those who view it through marital fidelity.

Marital Status – In this camp the four most common interpretations of the phrase "husband of one wife" include the following:

- The deacon will have only one wife in a lifetime, even after death of his spouse;
- The deacon is prohibited from being a polygamist;
- The deacon is prohibited from being divorced and/or remarried;
- A deacon candidate must be married.

Those in the first camp seem to be looking for a man who may "check the box" of the qualifications. The problem with any formulaic view of qualifications is that it creates the ability to technically meet the qualification but not the spirit of the qualification. In this case a man can "meet" the qualification but be in a loveless marriage. This approach veers toward legalism.

A good example is O'Donnell who dismisses three of the above views but holds that deacons are not to divorce.

> Some have taken this to mean that the deacon must be married. Although this is not the meaning, the married man would generally be more effective in his office than the unmarried man. Marriage is the most normal state of a man, and marriage would allow for broader relations in the church. Others have interpreted 'husbands of one wife' in a polygamous setting and interpret it to mean the husband of one wife at a time. Such a concept would open the office up to a man of multiple divorces, and this surely was not intended by Paul. The most natural interpretation of the phrase is that it prohibits divorce or any other marital infidelity in the deacon candidate. [30]

Marital Fidelity – The second camp views the "husband of one wife" phrase as a reference to marital fidelity, looking for a deacon candidate that lives out scriptural teaching of marriage. Here are the broader biblical principles:

- Genesis 2:18-24: The foundational truth in this passage is that God designed

---

[30] O'Donnell, *Handbook for Deacons*, 29.

marriage. The creation of woman out of man is unique among all of God's creation. When married, the man and the woman become one and are a unique family unit.
- 1 Corinthians 7:1-5: Intimate sexual relationship is only to be enjoyed in the context of marriage for the benefit of both man and woman.
- Ephesians 5:22-33: God's design for male headship in marriage and, for the couple, the call for sacrificial living unto each other. Specific to the man is the exhortation that, as a husband, he is to love and sacrifice for his wife as Christ did for the church.
- Matthew 19:3-9: These passages outline God's view on the sanctity of marriage and divorce.
- 1 Peter 3:8 says a husband should live in an understanding way with his wife --a command that wars men not to be overly authoritative leaders, but living two-as-one.

To clarify the proper biblical view is the second view, marital fidelity. A deacon is to be a "one-woman man" who is faithfully dedicated to his wife, who through the power of the Holy Spirit does not waiver in adhering to his marital vows or allow himself even to be enticed by other women. He is a man who takes seriously God's design for marriage, sexual intimacy with his wife and his position of headship and sacrifice for her unto God. To clarify further, a man does not have to be married to be a "one woman man." He must live a life that reflects sexual integrity and purity in his relational life, whether married or single.

10. *Managing their children and households well*

Similar to the qualification for elders, deacons are expected to raise their children in the fear and admonition of the Lord (Eph 6:4). They are to teach and model for their children clear biblical spiritual leadership so that the children cannot be accused of inappropriate behavior or considered rebellious (Titus 1:6).[31] Fatherhood was designed by God to be embraced where a father enjoys and looks forward to teaching spiritual things:

> Hear, Israel! The Lord is our God, the LORD is one! And you shall love the LORD your God with all your heart and with all your soul and with all your strength. These words, which I am commanding you today, shall be on your heart. And you shall repeat them diligently to your sons and speak of them when you sit in your house, when you walk on the road, when you lie down, and when you get up (Deut 6:4-7).

When a father neglects giving his children spiritual guidance and teaching them the way of the Lord, his children face doom like the children in Israel after Joshua's death:

> Then Joshua the son of Nun, the servant of the LORD, died at the age of 110. And they buried him in the territory of his inheritance in Timnath-heres, in the hill country of Ephraim, north of Mount Gaash.

---

[31] Van Dam, *The Deacon*, 69.

All that generation also were gathered to their fathers; and another generation rose up after them who did not know the LORD, nor even the work which He had done for Israel. Then the sons of Israel did evil in the sight of the LORD and served the Baals (Judges 2:8-11).

A deacon candidate needs to be faithfully raising his children to know and love God and his Word. The term "household" reaches beyond the relationship of a deacon candidate's wife and children. It includes having a proper biblical perspective as to extended family relationships, business relationships, financial relationships and financial dealings. The household of a deacon presents a comprehensive view of a deacon's life that is to be used to evaluate if he lives what he professes. Examining whether he is "holding to the mystery of the faith" looks at a deacon's general spiritual and theological maturity; examining whether he is "managing" his household considers at how he lives out his faith at home.

Deacons and Spiritual Gifts

Many authors reason that because Stephen and Phillip were gifted in evangelism, all deacons are to share in the ministry of the Word and provide spiritual leadership to the Body. The more pertinent analysis is that Steven and Philip were gifted in *service*. Had they not been, they would not have been appointed to help with the widows.

Yes, these two men were also gifted in evangelism. Both spoke to the Jerusalem crowds, with Stephen being the first Christian martyr as he was stoned to death for saying that Jesus was the promised Messiah (Acts 6:8-11). But Scripture clearly shows that the Acts 6 servants were ordained to care for the widows. If the apostles had ordained one of the seven, or all seven, into the ministry of the Word, then there would be merit in that view. But the apostles ordained the seven so that the *apostles* could concentrate on the ministry of the Word. First Timothy 3 clearly outlines church leadership: elders concentrate on the ministry of the Word and deacons are appointed to serve.

For a man to serve as a deacon, the gift of "service" or "helps" must be a primary area of gifting (1 Cor 12:28). That does not mean that is his only area of giftedness. Steven and Philip were gifted in service and obviously also were gifted in evangelism.

In our church, we have a deacon who is also a street evangelist. A couple of our other deacons teach in children's ministry. Another occasionally teaches in adult ministry. Their giftedness in these areas is very important to the church. However, these activities are ancillary and are not considered a part of the deacon roles. If a deacon is blessed to have gifts beyond service, these are to be exercised just as any other saint's giftedness is to be utilized within the church body—to serve one another and God for God's glory.

Not Every Servant is a Deacon

All believers are to be using their gifts in service to the church and its community of believers. However, that does not mean that all who serve in the church are deacons. There are some who take this view and do not realize the negative effect it has on the body and leadership. This view is harmful in two ways. First, it diminishes the qualifications outlined in Scripture for the office of deacon. Paul detailed a list of ten qualifications for deacons. Taken as a whole, these qualifications present a high bar of personal character qualities, attitude, and spiritual maturity. Not every believer is going to meet these. If a believer is led to believe that they meet these qualifications when they actually do not, they will likely become deceived about their spiritual condition.

Second, the view that every servant is a deacon diminishes the men who *do* meet the standard. Deacons are a significant part of the church leadership structure. In some ways they are the glue to help keep ministry and other operations properly moving. This is validated in Acts 6:7 when, after the seven were put into office, the following occurred: "And the word of God continued to increase, and the number of the disciples multiplied greatly in Jerusalem." This spiritually salutary circumstance verified that the process, selection, and men chosen were all in accordance with the Spirit's leading. The ministry of the Word was increased, meaning the apostles were freed to continue in their primary role as shepherds while the seven address a practical yet nevertheless critical problem in the church. To inappropriately elevate into leadership all those who serve and fail to properly identify true deacons creates dysfunction, which is usually followed by disharmony.

Summary

The selection process for choosing deacons is simple and straight-forward as outlined by Paul in 1 Timothy 3:10, "And let them also be tested first; then let them serve as deacons if they prove themselves blameless." This entails a four-step process:

1. Examine a deacon candidate to see if he meets the qualifications in vv. 8-12.
2. Examine their service, both past and present, to assess whether they would serve well alongside the elders.

The Selection Process and Qualifications

3. Examine their attitude and character while serving alongside other church servants.
4. "Let them serve." If a man is proven blameless through the evaluation, then let them serve. Ordain him to show the community of believers that this man is now a part of the formal leadership of the church.

Paul gave the local church elders autonomy in the above steps, insofar as how to engage the community of believers of the church in the selection process. Many point to Acts 6 in support of the belief that the church congregation has the authority to select its deacons. However, church leadership structure was not universalized until 1 Timothy 3, and, in fact, it is in 1 Timothy 3:10 that Paul details the process and gives elders autonomy over the selection process.

We also studied each of the qualifications given for deacons, with specific attention on aspiration for the office. Evaluating the nature of a man's desire to serve is a qualification missed by many authors but critical to the selection process and the execution of best practices in examining deacon candidates.

We also addressed the women in 1 Timothy 3:11. In this chapter we discussed the distinctive of the qualifications and the appropriateness of leaving the discussion of the women Paul is referring to for chapter eight.

A deacon candidate, as delineated in the Bible, is one that has been serving Christ's church, using God-given talents and giftedness to serve, and generally exhibiting an attitude, desire, and willingness to serve. When the elders have determined such a candidate meets these qualifications, works well with the elders and church members, notes that his past service shows him blameless and that he has been affirmed by the members, the Church has found a deacon.

"let them serve as deacons…"
1 Timothy 3:10b

6

The Ministry of a Deacon

What is the ministry of a deacon? Across the landscape of the universal church today there are numerous divergent views about the role and ministry of deacons. Below are just a few:

Deacons are spiritual leaders.[1]

Deacons are servants.[2]

Deacons are assistants to the elders.[3]

Deacons are not assistants of the elders but serve Christ for the good of the congregation.[4]

Deacons are those nearest to the needs of the people,

---

[1] Henry Webb, *Deacons: Servant Models in the Church* (Nashville, TN: B&H Publishing Group, 2001), 2.
[2] Benjamin Merkle, *40 Questions About Elders and Deacons* (Grand Rapids, MI: Kregel Publications, 2008), 238.
[3] Alexander Strauch, *Paul's Vision for the Deacons* (Littleton, CO: Lewis and Roth Publishers, 2017), 52.
[4] Cornelis Van Dam, *The Deacon: Biblical Foundations for Today's Ministry of Mercy* (Grand Rapids, MI: Reformation Heritage Books, 2016), 75.

spiritual or otherwise.[5]

Deacons are to protect the joy of the congregation by focusing on the poor, needy, lonely, and sick.[6]

Deacons are set apart for the ministry of love, justice, and service.[7]

Deacons are to support the ministry of the pastor.[8]

Deacons are to grow the ministry of the pastor.[9]

Deacons are to exercise general spiritual leadership.[10]

Deacons are to serve in the areas of pastoral leadership.[11]

Deacons are shepherds—they minister to the congregation, caring for the well-being of the flock.[12]

There is tremendous confusion and misunderstanding around the office of deacon. On one side of the spectrum, there is a narrow view of the role and purpose with a short list of specific duties usually around compassion ministry, quoting Acts 6 as the model. The other side claims deacons are shepherds and

---

[5] Harold Nichols, *The Work of the Deacon & Deaconess* (Valley Forge, PA: Judson Press, 2014), 29.
[6] Van Dam, *The Deacon*, 71-72.
[7] "The Ministry of a Deacon and Provisional Deacon," BOM Library, last modified January 2013, https://www.bomlibrary.org/wp-content/uploads/2015/06/Guide-for-Deacons.pdf.
[8] J.D. O'Donnell, *Handbook for Deacons* (Nashville, TN: Randall House Publications, 1973), 17.
[9] Robert Naylor, *The Baptist Deacon* (Nashville, TN: Broadman and Holman Publishers, 1955), 10.
[10] O'Donnel, *Handbook*, 73.
[11] Naylor, *The Baptist Deacon*, 10.
[12] Howard B. Foshee, *Now That You're a Deacon* (Nashville, TN: B&H Publishing Group, 1975), 15-16.

spiritual leaders of the church, with various other views in between.

It is obvious that from the list above the church has moved away from the simplicity that Paul laid out in 1 Timothy 3. Most of these views come from church traditions and denominational beliefs that have been foisted upon this apostolic template, smothering out its blessed instruction.

This chapter exposes wrong thinking about a deacon's ministry and provides a biblical foundation for a proper view.

The Ministry of Deacons

Christ's leadership structure for the church is elegantly simple. The Spirit initiated the office with the apostles in Acts 6 and universalized it with the apostle Paul in 1 Timothy 3. There are two offices, each with its own roles. They are both under Christ and directed by his Word for the benefit of the body. Both offices pertain only to the local church. There is no current office designated with authority over multiple churches. Bearing authority over multiple churches was the role of the apostles, and there are no apostles since the passing of the apostle John.

> ***Elders*** *are the overseers of the local church* (Acts 20:28). Elders are under-shepherds of Christ, overseeing all aspects of the church and responsible for every ministry of the church. The elders are responsible for overseeing everything from the finances of the church, to operations, to everything up to and including the teaching and preaching of the Word, which is their foremost responsibility.[13] This started

---

[13] Cliff McManis, *The Biblically-Driven Church* (Cupertino, CA: With All Wisdom Publications, 2016), 97-134.

with the apostles in the very first church (Acts 2:42; 4:32-35; 2 Tim 4:2; 1 Tim 4:11-16; 1 Peter 5:1), and continues in the New Testament and today with elders (1 Tim 4:11-16; 2 Tim 4:2). When additional management servants are needed, deacons should be appointed (Acts 6:6; 1 Tim 3:10).

Deacons *serve the body of the church through elder-appointed tasks* (Acts 6:6; 1 Tim 3:10). Deacons do not choose where they serve. The Bible does not prescribe tasks to deacons. The ministry of the deacon is simply to serve where the elders direct, as long as it is not a biblically-defined elder task.

Two offices: (1) the overseers bear the responsibility of all areas of the church; and (2) the deacons are appointed to serve and manage. In Acts 4, the apostles oversaw and managed the entirety of the ministry including the care of the widows. The ministry of the widows required so much attention it began to take away from the apostles' primary duties. So, the apostles in Acts 6 appointed men to handle the task. The same is true for the deacons established by Paul, with one modification. Deacons carry out any service tasks appointed by the elders for the needs of the body. This allows the elders to keep focused on the ministry of the Word so they would not be distracted by practical needs that required attention (just as the apostles in Acts 6). There is nothing in Acts 6 or the rest of the New Testament that establishes that deacons can only serve widows or the needy. Interestingly, Paul did not create a special title or word for this office of service. He used the noun *daikon* which means "a servant" or "to serve." It was a straightforward, well-known job with a simple title.

The two offices in this model work together to address

the needs of the congregation for God's glory, and the result is captured in Acts 6:7: "And the word of God continued to increase, and the number of the disciples multiplied greatly"(ESV).

Hard Boundaries and Autonomy
Paul gave the local church a specific set of qualifications, roles, and duties for its elders. For deacons, he provided a set of qualifications and roles, leaving the elders freedom in the selection process and appointing specific tasks to the deacons. Paul did not give the elders flexibility to add to the qualifications of deacons, or to expand the role of a deacon.

The qualifications of deacons were examined in chapter five. The qualifications between the two offices (elders and deacons) are similar, and a cursory review might lead some to believe there are no real differences. This could be an underlying reason why, over the centuries, spiritual leadership and other similar tasks have been added to the deacon's role. However, further study shows there are some major differences and key distinctives between the qualifications of the two offices.

The primary qualifications that separate elders and deacons are teaching, preaching (1 Tim 3:2), counseling, and exhortation (Titus 1:9). It is the elders who are to minister the Word of God. Deacons serve and help manage other servants. Herein you find an elegant, clear, and simple division of labor.

Can Deacons Teach?
The office of deacon does not have qualifications *requiring* them to teach. A deacon may have a personal spiritual gift of teaching (Rom 12:6-8), but their role doesn't require that they possess this gift. Every believer receives at least one spiritual gift (1 Cor 12:3), and all deacons have the gift of service (Rom

12:7; 1 Pet 4:10-11). They may also have other gifts, including the gift of teaching (1 Cor 12:11).

The gift of teaching varies in skill and depth, from teaching a children's class, to leading an in-depth inductive Bible study, to teaching through a book of the Bible. It is not uncommon to find deacons who have the gift of teaching at one of these levels. Stephen and Philip, for example, had personal spiritual gifts beyond their service to the widows (Acts 6, 8). Both men performed wonders and miracles, both preached the Word with boldness.

A deacon who also has the gift of teaching is not necessarily qualified to be an elder. As we have seen, elders must be able to preach, counsel, and exhort (Titus 1:9) across the whole counsel of God's Word. So, a deacon who has the gift of teaching may become an elder based on the fullness of elder qualifications.

Can a Church Operate Without Elders or Deacons?

At a panel discussion John MacArthur was asked, "When does a church that is being planted actually become a functioning church?" MacArthur responded, "When there is a plurality of elders." He pointed to Paul's instruction to Titus 1:5 and Acts 14:23 to appoint elders—plural—in their churches. In Paul's letters, when he addressed the elders of a church, the office of elders was always in the plural form. It is clear from Scripture that Christ's church is to have a plurality of spiritual leaders. So, a church plant may start with a single elder, but as Paul asserts, to operate properly, multiple elders are needed to serve his sheep.

Deacons serve the church body through elder-appointed tasks, so, by definition, the church and elders exist *before* deacons. As seen in the first church in Acts 1-6, the church began and was fully operational under the apostles (elders/spiritual leaders of the church). In Acts 1-5 there were no ordained servants to serve until a ministry (for widows) arose that began to take the apostles away from their primary task. It was then that the apostles appointed men to serve. So, a church must have elders to properly function, but it does not immediately require deacons. The apostle Paul asserted the same as he urged Titus to appoint elders in every church. Spiritual-leaders (elders) are required in every church. Servant-leaders (deacons) are appointed as elders as needed.

However, a church should not exist very long before it has need of deacons. The Jerusalem church was less than two years old before the apostles saw the need for qualified men to help serve. Churches have many needs that pull elders away from their spiritual oversight. Any church that is beyond its infancy should have deacons.

Dismissal of a Deacon

There are three reasons to dismiss a deacon from his office. The first is unrepentant sin. If anyone within the church—deacon or elder included—has been caught living in unrepentant sin, the proper way to address the sin is through the four-step process Christ gave in Matthew 18:15-20. If they do not repent through the first three steps—(1) v. 15 one-on-one confrontation; (2) v. 16 confrontation with two or more members; (3) v. 17a formal rebuke by the church—then if they don't respond (v. 17b) the deacon shall be removed from the church and treated as a pagan or tax collector. These are Christ's own words—his process for dealing with sin in the church. This first reason for dismissal is straightforward.

The second reason for dismissal is not as straightforward and requires much prayer and wisdom among the elders. If a deacon has lived in unrepentant sin for a period of time but somewhere in the Matthew 18 process there is repentance and restoration to the body, then a good thing has been accomplished. However, if the reputation of the man as viewed by the body or elders has been damaged, he may need to be dismissed as a deacon. I have seen deacons who had no previous issue with alcohol be overcome by the temptation, even one receiving a DUI. An issue with alcohol is not easily or quickly reversed. Setbacks are common. This is an example of when the elders need to pray and discuss what is most honoring to the Lord—even when the deacon repents and is working on the addiction. Dismissal needs to be considered in such circumstances, not because he sinned, but because he did not faithfully get help before the sin rose to the level of being out of control. This is an issue of faithfulness and staying "above reproach" (1 Tim 3:10). Elders need to consider how the circumstances will affect both the body and others in leadership.

The two offices of leadership have strict qualifications for character and holiness that are to be upheld and modeled to the body. Christ established these standards for his leaders. Christ knows well that as men we are not perfect, and we should not pretend to be. Such behavior is Pharisaical. All men are sinful, and, as leaders, elders, and deacons, we need to model holiness and deal with personal sin quickly (Matt 5:23-24), keeping short accounts and staying accountable to one another.

The third reason to dismiss a deacon is the loss of integrity in his service. This is when the deacon is no longer blameless in his service. This is when they are not properly fulfilling their duties or when they are lacking in one or more of their qualifications listed in 1 Timothy 3:8-12. As an example, he could be undignified in how he is managing areas of service and the people in the body he serves; consistently responding in anger, or being demeaning, passive-aggressive, micromanaging, or other ungodly behavior. He could be wavering in his faith or he may be failing at managing his family. Christ wants men who will respond to the prompting of their conscience and the Holy Spirit when issues occur. If a pattern has become evident that questions the qualifications and character of a deacon, the elders need to confront him and confirm all details. The elders need to pray with and counsel the deacon, urging him to properly respond. Ultimately, elders need to do what is best for the congregation, which may require dismissal of the deacon but still caring for him as shepherds.

Elders should be overseeing deacons and their ministry, keeping them accountable. This is a practical reason why deacons are to be tested first before being installed (1 Tim 3:10).

Leave of Absence

A leave of absence is not a dismissal from office due to sin or failure to meet the character qualifications. Rather, this is when issues of life demand the deacon to turn his full attention away from church service for a period of time. These are typically family or practical personal issues. In our church a deacon's wife had life-threatening cancer. They had two children—one in high school, and one in middle school. He took a leave of absence to care for his wife and family. Another one of our deacons helped care for his sister-in-law who suffered from a debilitating disease. When that disease reached its later stages, he took a leave to help with the added needs surrounding her care. Others have taken leave when dealing with serious career or business issues that required an extended amount of time and focused attention.

A good deacon knows his ministry and knows the proper balance it has with his other life duties. When life becomes unbalanced, there are times that God will provide the strength to continue forward (Eph 3:14-19). There are also times the Holy Spirit will guide a man to rebalance by taking things off the scales.

Elders may need to help deacons assess and pray about a leave of absence. Many times, deacons are reluctant to take a needed leave, believing in their call and that God will provide the needed strength and the ability to continue their service. Though this could be true, it could also be true that it is best for the man to reprioritize and take a leave for a period of time. This is another reason elders must oversee the ministry of their deacons, helping to watch and pray for them and their ministry.

Teach Biblical Leadership

In the previous chapter, I quoted Judges 2:10 with reference to the importance of a father instructing his children in the Lord: "There arose another generation after them who did not know the LORD or the work that he had done for Israel." This principle of fathers modeling spiritual leadership by instructing their children also applies to the church. If biblical leadership is to be understood and valued, then it has to be taught. As we saw in the last chapter, Paul had five "trustworthy sayings" he taught in his churches. These five things were regularly repeated as constant reminders of the core of the gospel, doctrine, and leadership. The apostle Paul taught his churches biblical leadership. Paul instructed his young pastors, Timothy and Titus, who were ministering after him, to teach biblical leadership (2 Tim 3:14).

Today, we have numerous church leadership structures, roles, practices, and traditions that do not match what Christ prescribed for his churches. Christ's structure is elegant and simple which brings harmony to the body when implemented correctly as seen in Acts 6:7. A revival of New Testament leadership structure is needed in our churches worldwide.

Summary

Deacons should be qualified, Spirit-filled men established to manage and serve the body, all for the glory of God through delegated tasks from the elders. Acts 6 initiated the office of deacon, with servants dedicated to serving widows. First Timothy 3 universalized the office, providing elders tremendous autonomy to determine the scope of a deacon's ministry.

Some ask, "If a deacon's role is simply service, then why aren't all church servants considered deacons?" This is best answered with the situation in Acts 6. The issue was not the lack of people willing to serve. Acts 4:4 tells us the church was in excess of 5,000 men (probably over 12-15,000) total people with women and children) who were serving and sacrificing for one another. There were people helping to serve the widows. The issue had to do with the need for wise, Spirit-filled management and fairness. This occasion required a specialized need of exceptional and mature service for a unique task for a problem that confronted the young church on a broad scale. The church was vulnerable to wholesale division. Hence, the qualifications established by the apostles.

There are many men and women who serve their local church faithfully across a large range of needs. God gifts and talents his people to serve one another, teach, preach, train, disciple, sing, play instruments, and much more. All believers are called to serve in their local church. However, not all servants are called to formal church leadership.

There are three reasons to dismiss a deacon. The first is for unrepentant sin that should be confronted with the process Christ established in Matthew 18. The second and third are not as straightforward and need deep thought and prayer by the elders. Both of these are not necessarily based in sin but deal with the qualifications of maintaining a good reputation and being blameless in carrying out their duties. Deacons may also take a leave of absence to focus on personal, work, or family matters that require their undivided attention.

"For those who serve well as deacons gain **a good standing** for themselves and also **great confidence** in the faith that is in Christ Jesus."
1 Timothy 3:13

7

Christ's Promise to Deacons

God gives two special promises to deacons in 1 Timothy 3:13. It is easy to quickly read over the verse and not appreciate the depth of the promises. The promises of Christ are never small or insignificant. Christ gives two promises to deacons who serve well. First, they will have good standing, and second, they will have great confidence in their faith.

A Good Standing
The first promise to faithful deacons is that they will have a good standing. Men who have been examined, found blameless, and appointed to service are tremendously valuable to the church. The harmony of the church seen in Acts 6:7 occurs today when elders and deacons follow biblical leadership and bless the church. Faithful deacons are the humble servants managing appointed, necessary tasks from the elders for the body to the glory of God (1 Cor 10:31). They often serve behind the scenes. At other times they are more visible, helping to manage groups of people to achieve necessary tasks for the church.

When faithful deacons are serving in this manner, Christ

promises they will have a good standing, specifically, within their church body. The saints will witness the proper operational harmony of Christ's two-office leadership structure resulting in the spiritual growth of the church. When these things are clearly manifested, a deacon will be esteemed in an appropriate manner. He will have a good reputation and have the respect of the church body.

The context of having a "good standing" is primarily within the local church and within the community of believers. It can, however, flow over into other areas of a deacon's life. The strong moral character of a deacon will be respected in the workplace, around the neighborhood, by extended family, friends, and all across the unbelieving world he touches. At the same time, the world is fickle in its estimations of moral excellence. Biblical character can also be held against a believer. This corrupt world will accept a moral man one day and reject him another. Regardless of the world's view of a faithful deacon, Christ's promise remains. He will be blessed by God and esteemed by his local church.

Great Confidence in the Faith

The second promise is "great confidence in the faith." Why would Christ give his deacons who serve well an increased confidence? Sin is always trying to divide saints against each other. Church leaders are prime targets (1 Tim 3:6-7). If Satan can weave divisiveness within elders and deacons, and thereby create splits within leadership, then Satan can gain a foothold and divide the church.

Satan may target a deacon personally. If he can get a church leader to disqualify himself, this too can wreak havoc in the local church. A deacon or elder who mishandles alcohol, has an affair, or any other compromise of the qualifications, will bring on a tremendous burden and sadness to their church and may create a flood of problems.

It is important for a church and its leaders to have unity and not allow Satan to gain a foothold. Christ knows that Satan will attack his leaders. Christ strengthens deacons for the attack by having the Holy Spirit embolden their faith. "A great confidence in the faith that is in Christ Jesus" (1 Tim 3:13) is a bountiful gift for deacons. A great and supernatural confidence in faith helps deacons face issues that will inevitably come.

Christ knows the weight and stress of leadership. He knows how Satan will attack his leaders (Luke 22:31; 1 Pet 5:8). Christ gives a great promise that his deacons will be honored by the saints of the local church and be given supernaturally strong faith to withstand the trials of this fallen world and the challenges that Satan brings.

"Their **wives** likewise must be dignified, not slanderers, but sober-minded, faithful in all things."
(ESV)

"**Women** must likewise be dignified, not malicious gossips, but temperate, faithful in all things."
(NASB)
1 Timothy 3:11

"I commend to you our sister Phoebe, who is a **servant** of the church which is at Cenchrea."
(NASB)

"I commend to you our sister Phoebe, a **deacon** of the church in Cenchreae."
(NIV)
Romans 16:1

8

Who are the Women in 1 Timothy 3:11?

As our study has shown, there has been much confusion about the office of deacon over 2,000 years of church history. This confusion includes the interpretation of 1 Timothy 3:11, where there is much debate about the role and identification of the women Paul is writing about.

The interpretation of this verse and the surrounding passage is difficult. Several reasons account for the interpretative challenge regarding this verse:

1. How this verse should be translated is highly disputed. The difficulty with translation is centered on the Greek word *gune* which can be translated "women" or "wives." There is no direct word for "wife" in the Greek. Context determines the translation.
2. There is limited information from Paul surrounding the role and identity of the "women" mentioned in this verse; it is somewhat cryptic.

3. Idiosyncratic syntactical and literary features pose a challenge for the exegete.
4. The many diverse and often contradictory ways in which the church has treated the role of the women in 3:11 for almost 2,000 has also affected exegetes and commentators; some have allowed past practices of church history to infect and affect their current interpretation of the passage.

All four of these daunting features play out to varying degrees in translation, interpretation and in application, thus compounding the challenge of discovering who the females are in 3:11.

Greek Text and Bible Translations

To unpack this complex verse let's start by looking at the Greek text and various English Bible translations.

The Greek text of 1 Timothy 3:11

Γυναῖκας ὡσαύτως σεμνάς μὴ διαβόλους

[women/wives] [likewise] [reverent] [not diabolical]

νηφαλίους πιστὰς ἐν πᾶσιν

[clear-minded] [faithful] [in] [all things]

The various English translations fall roughly into two broad camps. One camp prefers to translate the main Greek noun in the sentence (γυναῖκας, *gunaikos*) as "women" and the second camp translate the word as "wives." Either translation is permissible on the face of it, but the different renderings yield significantly different interpretations and implications.

Who are the Women in 1 Timothy 3:11?

Translations that render gunaikos as "women"

> NSAB and LSB "Women must likewise be dignified, not malicious gossips, but temperate, faithful in all things"
>
> NIV "In the same way, the women are to be worthy of respect, not malicious talkers but temperate and trustworthy in everything"

Translations that render gunaikos as "wives":

> NKJV – Likewise, their wives must be reverent, not slanderers, temperate, faithful in all things
>
> ESV – Their wives likewise must be dignified, not slanderers, but sober-minded, faithful in all things
>
> CSB – Wives, likewise, should be worthy of respect, not slanderers, self-controlled, faithful in everything
>
> NET – Likewise also their wives must be dignified, not slanderous, temperate, faithful in every respect

The various translations make immediately apparent the challenge that confronts the Bible interpreter. For example, even the great reformer, John Calvin, seems to have had a run-in with this knotty passage as he modified his view about how the verse should be understood. In his *Institutes* he supported the view of female deacons.[1] But later in his ministry, he implies that men only are deacons.[2] Similarly, others throughout church history have wrestled with this passage to determine

---

[1] John Calvin, *Institutes of the Christian Religion*, translated by Henry Beveridge (Peabody, MA: Hendrickson Publishers, 2008), Bk 4, Ch 3, Sec 9; cf. Bk 4, Ch 13, Sec 19.

[2] John Calvin, *Commentaries on the Epistles to Timothy, Titus, and Philemon, Vol. XXI*, translated by William Pringle (Grand Rapids, MI: Baker Book House, 2003), 87.

Christ's will for his church, and like Calvin, some have changed views over time.

Before looking at the various competing interpretations of 1 Timothy 3:11, it is helpful to consider how *gune* is used throughout the New Testament. The word translated as "women" or "wives" in 3:11 is *gunaikas,* the accusative form of the Greek noun *gune*. *Gune* and its various forms are used at least 217 times in the New Testament and is translated primarily as either "woman/women" or "wife/wives" depending on the context. It can refer to "any adult female" including "virgins" or it can mean a "wife."[3] In some contexts where it occurs the meaning of the translation is undisputed, whereas other occurrences are highly debated. Consider a sampling of its common usages:

1. Occasions where *gune* clearly means women in general, including virgins, married and non-married women:
   "everyone who looks at **a woman** [*gunaika*] with lust for her has already committed adultery with her in his heart" (Matt 5:28; cf. 14:21; 15:38).

2. Occasions where *gune* clearly means a wife, a married woman only:
   "everyone who divorces **his wife** [*ten gunaika*], except for *the* reason of unchastity, makes her commit adultery" (Matt 5:32; cf. 14:3; 18:25; 19:3).

3. Occasions where *gune* refers to a specific woman, such as Eve, the first female:
   "And *it was* not Adam *who* was deceived, but **the**

---

[3] Walter Bauer, *A Greek-English Lexicon of the New Testament and Other Early Christian Literature* (Chicago, IL: University of Chicago Press, 2001), 168.

woman [*he...gune*] being deceived, fell into transgression" (1 Tim 2:14; cf. 1 Cor 11:8-9).

4. An occasion where *gune* refers to widows:
"A widow is to be put on the list only if she is not less than sixty years old, *having been* the wife [*gune*] of one man" (1 Tim 5:9).

5. Occasions where the word *gune* can be translated as "woman" or "wife":
"But because of immoralities, each man is to have his own wife [*ten...gunaika*], and each

[*hekaste*] *woman* is to have her own husband" (1 Cor 7:2; cf. 1 Cor 14:34).

First Timothy 3:11 falls into category five, unfortunately, meaning the word *gune* is not as specific in terms of how it is used as seen in categories 1-4 above. There is limited exegetical data to go by. This is the challenge. There is unavoidable ambiguity. As such, there are competent Greek scholars lined up on all sides of the various views. Grammar or vocabulary alone does not resolve this matter. The answer is best surmised based on contextual considerations along with syntactical and grammatical factors which will be considered later. Further, it is important to note that Paul used the word *gune* frequently in his epistles, at least sixty-four times. It was a common word. He used it in seven of his thirteen epistles: one time in Romans, forty times in 1 Corinthians, one time in Galatians, ten times in Ephesians, two times in Colossians, once in Titus and nine times in 1 Timothy. In the book that concerns us here, 1 Timothy, Paul uses the term *gune* in at least three ways:

1. Women – It refers to all adult Christian women in the church in 2:9-12.
2. Wife – In 2:14 the term refers to Eve. In 3:2 it refers to the wife of an overseer. In 3:12 it refers to the wife of a deacon.
3. Widow – And in 5:9 it is used in reference to a Christian widow.

Various Views

Now that we have set forth the various English translations and given some background to the usage of the word *gune*, it is time to consider the various interpretations typically offered by Bible commentators followed by short evaluations of each view. The disputed females (*gunaikos*) of 1 Timothy 3:11 have been understood in at least seven different ways:

1. women in general;[4]
2. women assistants of the deacons;[5]
3. women assistants of the elders[6]
4. deaconesses[7]
5. women deacons;[8]
6. deacons' wives;[9]

---

[4] Adam Clarke, *Clarke's Commentary, Vol. VI: Romans to Revelation* (New York: Abingdon Press, 1900), 597.
[5] William Hendriksen, *New Testament Commentary: Thessalonians, Timothy and Titus* (Grand Rapids, MI: Baker Book House, 1990), 133.
[6] Robert H. Gundry, *Commentary on the New Testament* (Peabody, MA: Hendrickson Publishers, 2010), 781, 838.
[7] Donald Guthrie, *Tyndale New Testament Commentaries: The Pastoral Epistles* (Grand Rapids, MI: Eerdmans Publishing Company, 1980), 85; John MacArthur, *The MacArthur New Testament Commentary: 1 Timothy* (Chicago, IL: Moody Publishers, 1995), 130; Gordon D. Fee, *New International Biblical Commentary: 1 and 2 Timothy, Titus* (Peabody, MA: Hendrickson Publishers, 1988), 88.
[8] John Koessler, "1 Timothy," *The Moody Bible Commentary*, ed. Michael Rydelink and Michael Vanlaningham (Chicago, IL: Moody Publishers, 2014), 1899; Harold Nichols, *The Work of the Deacon & Deaconess* (Valley Forge, PA: Judson Press, 2014), 4.
[9] A. Duane Litfin, *The Bible Knowledge Commentary: New Testament Edition*, ed. John F. Walvoord and Roy B. Zuck (Wheaton, IL: Victor Books, 1986), 738; Alexander Strauch, *The New Testament Deacon* (Littleton, CO: Lewis & Roth Publishers, 1992), 112-131.

7. the wives of both elders and deacons.[10]

Women in general
Proponents of this view believe Paul interrupts the male deacon's qualifications to introduce four qualifications for all Christian women in general, similar to what Paul did in 1 Timothy 2:9-15. From this perspective *gunaikos* is translated as "women" are refers to all the adult females in the church. This view can be dismissed based on syntax. The use of the adverb "likewise" militates against such an interpretation. Using "likewise" makes the reference to the women parallel with the deacons just mentioned, men who constitute a specific subset within a larger group of all men.[11] Additionally, the use of "likewise" throughout 1 Timothy 3:1-13 shows it as one unit of thought on church leadership.

Women assistants to the deacons
Proponents of this view believe the women are to assist deacons in ministry to other women, the poor, and those in need. They do not believe women are to have an official title of "woman deacon" or "deaconess." Rather, they are "women helpers," aiding the deacons in their service. This view invokes "syntax" as being in its favor. The verb phrase "must be" [*dei…einai*] from 3:2 is said to be carried forward in application to the deacons in 3:8 ("likewise the deacons *must be*") and to the women in 3:11("likewise the women *must be*). As such, "One and the same verb coordinates the three: the overseer, deacons, women." At the same time this view says the women in this distinct group and role do not constitute an official office in the church because Paul just said in the previous

---

[10] Calvin, *Commentaries on the Epistles,* 87.
[11] Alexander Strauch, *Paul's Vision for the Deacons* (Littleton, CO: Lewis and Roth Publishers, 2017), 121.

chapter, 1 Timothy 2:1-15, that women cannot exercise authority in the church. And to illustrate this unique group of women who do not constitute a church office but who have a distinct role as auxiliary helpers to the deacons, Paul supposedly strategically "wedges" them in "parenthetically" between the qualifications of deacon.[12] This view is in the minority for a reason, namely it *lacks* exegetical and contextual support. The passage does not call the women "helpers" or "assistants." In fact, the passage does not even assign them a duty. There is no verb describing what they do. Hendriksen insists these women were called to "help the poor and needy." But the text does not say that. The text only describes them with four-character qualifications. Paul specifies duties for women in the corporate assembly in 1 Timothy 2 and in 1 Timothy 5. There are no duties prescribed here.

Women assistants to the elders
This view holds that *diaconon* in 3:8 should not be translated as "deacons" but in its most general and normal usage as "servant" or more specifically as "assistants." The word "deacon" is merely an empty transliteration providing no description of what this term actually entails. Prominent Greek scholar, Robert Gundry explains: "Traditional English translations read 'deacons' instead of 'assistants,' but 'deacons' obscures that these people are to serve the supervisors [i.e., overseers/elders] by assisting them."[13] He further notes, "The traditional translation 'deacons' doesn't adequately identify the activities of these people."[14] Gundry also argues that the term "overseer" [*episkopon*] of 3:2 is better translated as "supervisor,"

---

[12] William Hendriksen, *New Testament Commentary: Thessalonians, Timothy and Titus* (Grand Rapids, MI: Baker Book House, 1990), 132-133.
[13] Gundry, *Commentary*, 838.
[14] Gundry, *Commentary*, 781.

not as "bishop," which, similar to the word "deacon," is more of a quasi-transliteration and not an explanatory translation of the word. With respect to the "women" of 3:11 Gundry says they are "assistants" to the supervisors just as the male assistants are. So the women are not assistants to the male deacons, the wives of the deacons, nor those serving in a formal office called "Deaconess." He goes on in explaining his exegesis of 3:11 in the context:

> Romans 16:1 designates a woman named Phoebe as an assistant; and since 'assistant' had no grammatically feminine form in Greek but occurred for females as well as males, to make plain a reference to female assistants Paul uses 'women' and inserts a snippet concerning them before reverting to male assistants in 3:12-13. That no similar snippet was inserted for female supervisors agrees with Paul's requiring women to learn 'in total subjection' and 'not to exercise authority over a man' (2:11-12), and that he doesn't require a female assistant to have an aptitude for teaching any more than he required male assistants to have that aptitude agrees with his not permitting a woman to teach a man (2:12). "Respectable" [*semnas*] matches exactly the requirement that male assistants be 'respectable' (3:8).[15]

Despite Gundry's creativity and novelty, while trying to deal with the text, his view leaves too many questions unanswered, especially the question of why male assistants are given nine qualifications while the female assistants only have four when

---

[15] Gundry, *Commentary*, 838-839.

they are supposedly fulfilling the same service or role.

Deaconesses
Proponents of this view see women as servants or ministers on a separate level, not fully equal to male deacons. They blend the role of women addressed by Paul in 1 Timothy 2:10 with the women in 3:11. Proponents explain that these women serve but do not assert leadership over men. Therefore, they are not fully equal to male deacons. Nevertheless, their role of service is vital and appropriate for the constitution of a woman. In practice, these women have a formal but limited role when compared to deacons as they focus on serving other women, children, and fellowship of the church. Some who hold this view attempt to buttress their position by arguing that 1 Timothy 5:9-10 is a complimentary reference to deaconesses.[16] There are several issues with this position. One of the most significant is the creation of a third tier of leadership. The context of the 1 Timothy 3:1-13 is church leadership and establishes both elders and male deacons. This view (including the two previous views: assistants to the elders, assistants to the deacons) creates a third tier of leadership not addressed anywhere else in the New Testament. If these women are simply servants, as most proponents espouse, then why is v. 11 in a passage on leadership? If simply servants, then how are they different than other servants? Why is the word for servant (noun or verb) not used in v. 11.

Women servants have been a vital element of church life since the first century. The New Testament showcases numerous women servants that served Christ, the apostles, and local churches:

---

[16] Merrill F. Unger, *The New Unger's Bible Dictionary* (Chicago, IL: Moody Publishers, 2006), 288-289.

Who are the Women in 1 Timothy 3:11?

Mary the mother of Jesus – Acts 1:14
Mary Magdalene – Luke 24:10
Mary, the mother of James – Luke 24:10
Joanna – Luke 24:10
Salome – Mark 15:40-41
Anna the prophetess – Luke 2:36-38
Joanna and Susanna – Luke 8:2-3
Martha – Luke 10:38
Mary of Bethany – Luke 10:39
Tabitha (Dorcas) – Acts 9:36-42
Mary, Mother of JohnMark – Acts 12:12
Rhoda – Acts 12:13-15
Lydia – Acts 16:40
Priscilla – Acts 18:18
Daughters of Philip, prophetesses – Acts 21:9
Mary of Rome – Rom 16:6
Phoebe – Rom 16:1
Junia – Rom 16:7
Tryphaena and Tryphosa – Rom 16:12
Persis – Rom 16:12
Mother of Rufus – Rom 16:13
Julia and Sister of Nereus – Rom 16:15
Chloe – 1 Cor 1:11
Eudia and Syntych – Phil 4:2-3
Claudia – 2 Tim 4:21
Apphia – Philem 1:2

Men and women servants of Christ's church play a critical role in serving one another and building up the body of Christ (1 Cor 12). Serving one another is fundamental for all Christians. It comes from the new command Christ gave to the disciples the night before his death in the upper room after dismissing

Judas. All believers are to love and serve one another. This will be a witness to the world (John 13:34-35).

From early church history, women have served the church across a variety of ministries ranging from nursery, children's ministry, women's ministry, music, and fellowship meals to Bible studies, teaching, discipleship, counseling, financial support and more. If the elders of a local church wish to designate areas for women to serve and desire to call them deaconesses, it is within the autonomy of those elders to do so. In 1 Timothy 2:12, a few verses before Paul establishes church leadership structure (1 Tim 3:1-13), he does not allow women to teach or have authority over men. If local elders choose to have deaconesses, a proper scope of their role needs to be established. There needs to be clear communication that their roles do not include being a church leader in a formal office recognized by Scripture or being equal to the position of male deacons.

Women deacons

Proponents of this view see Paul clearly introducing the qualifications of women deacons. They believe the context of the passage shows male and female deacons as equals in all duties and roles. Some who hold this view are strongly opposed to the term "deaconess," believing that both male and female deacons are equal in their positions and role.[17] This is the most egalitarian view.

Verses 8 through 10 provide six-character qualifications of male deacons. Proponents of this view believe the four-character qualifications in v. 11 for the women are the same as those for the men. But the specific grammar reveals that only one qualification uses the same Greek word. The remaining

---

[17] Nichols, *The Work of the Deacon*, 4.

three-character qualifications have a commonality of subject and Greek root word. This leads some commentators to conclude the character qualifications are equal to male deacons. Other commentators view the differences in the Greek words illustrate the essence of the female character qualities as different than male. Below are the two passages followed by a breakdown of the vocabulary.

> Deacons likewise must be dignified, not double-tongued, not addicted to much wine, not greedy for dishonest gain. They must hold the mystery of the faith with a clear conscience. These men must also first be tested; then have them serve as deacons if they are beyond reproach (1 Tim 3:8-10).

> Women/wives likewise must be dignified, not slanderers, but sober-minded, faithful in all things (1 Tim 3:11).

If 1 Timothy 3:8-12 is endorsing women deacons, then females have a different set of qualifications than males. This contradicts the primary view of this position that men and women deacons are equal in all qualifications.

- Verses 8-10 clearly identify six qualifications for men, with v. 12 identifying two more for qualifications, v. 1/v. 10 has the qualification of aspiration a total of nine qualifications
- Verse 10 calls for thorough examination of male deacons and the qualification of them passing that test. No such examination is required of the women in v. 11.

Comparison of Male and Female Qualifications			
Verse	Male Qualification	Verse	Female Qualification
8	Dignified, Greek *semnous* – to be revered, respected, dignified.	11	Dignified, Greek *semnas* – to be revered, respected, dignified.
Same as word in both verses			
8	Not double-tongued (*dilogous* – deceitful, saying one thing and meaning another, or making different representations to different people about the same thing).	11	Not slanderers (*diabolous* – a false accuser, or unjustly criticizing, maligning, slanderer).

Dilogous – Strong's Concordance 1351. This is the only occurence of this word in the New Testament.
Diabolous – Strong's Concordance 1228. The word root is *diaballo* used 37 times in the New Testament – 34 times translated as devil, 3 times translated as malicious gossip/not slanderers.

8	Not addicted to much wine, Greek *me oino pollo* – not desiring great amounts of wine, sober.	11	Sober-minded, Greek *nephalious* – sober, not intoxicated, temperate.
8	Not greedy for dishonest gain, Greek *prosechontas me aischrokerdeis* – not devoted to the pursuit of nor desirous of greedy gain.	N/A	There is no qualification listed for women

Verse 8 "not addicted to much wine" and verse 11 "being sober-minded" are the same. One being stated from the positive "being sober" one from the negative "not addicted…"

Verse 8 "not greedy for dishonest gain" speaks to the motivation and heart of a deacon. There is no qualification listed in verse 11 for women.

9	Hold the mystery of the faith with a clear conscience, Greek *echontas to, mysterion tes pisteos en kathara syneidesei* – this is holding to the deep mysteries of the faith provided by Paul throughout the New Testament including incarnation, indwelling of the Spirit, the church, the rapture and the gospel itself.	11	Faithful in all things, Greek *pistas en pasin* – faithfulness in all endeavors, enduring through issues to complete tasks in excellence as unto God.

These verses have a commonality of the same root word "faith" (*peitho*) as the primary word in the main phrase. For comparison purposes they are parallel. Verse 9 speaks to a deacon living out his faith that is open and obvious to the body, a genuine faith not manufactured (with a clear conscience). Verse 11 speaks of women being faithful with their duties all for the glory of God. Both verses speak of faith-based living but with differing elements. A deacon's character lives a walk of faith that is not hypocritical while the woman's focus is on the endurance to complete all things in excellence for God's glory.

10	These men must also first be tested; then have them serve as deacons if they are beyond reproach	N/A	There is no qualification listed for women

Verse 10 a man is to be tested and shown to be above reproach before he is to be installed as a deacon. This is a verse is both a qualification for a deacon and helps to direct the selection process of a deacon as discussed in chapter five. There is no qualification listed in verse 11 for women.

- Verse 11 clearly identifies four qualifications for women.
- One qualification has the same meaning for men and women but use different words – not addicted to wine v. 8, sober v. 11.
- One qualification has the same root word of faith. Verse 8 speaks of "holding to the mystery of the faith," while v. 11 speaks to endurance of the faith. These are parallel but not exactly the same.
- Male qualifications that are unaddressed include the following: not greedy for dishonest gain, testing, being a one women man, managing the household well, and aspiring to the position of deacon (see chapter five).

Since the set of qualifications for men are not equal to those of the women and there is no examination of the women it would follow that if women are to be deacons, Paul would then describe the position and role of the women. There is no clear description of this role in 1 Timothy 3 or elsewhere in the New Testament. This is the main weakness of this view. If men and women are to be deacons with no difference based on gender, then Paul would not have given a separate set of qualifications for the women. He would have made it clear.

Deacons' wives

Proponents of this view see verse 11 as the qualifications for the wife of a deacon, meaning a deacon must have a godly wife, a wife that is dignified, not a slanderer, sober-minded and faithful. This view fits in the flow of the passage grammatically and contextually. Verses 8-9 are personal character qualifications of the deacon. Verse 10 requires a deacon to be tested and found blameless before being installed. Verse 11 provides character qualities needed from the deacon's wife, and verse 12 gives qualities are required in his marriage and family.[18] This view brings the total of deacon qualifications to ten.

However, many argue that the interpretation of verse 11 being a "deacon's wife" is invalid since there are no qualifications for an elder's wife. Opponents conclude the absence of an elder's wife's qualifications in the 1 Timothy 3 passage or anywhere else in Scripture invalidates the view that verse 11 applies to a deacon's wife. Therefore, they say verse 11 must be endorsing women deacons or deaconesses. This argument from silence is not based on using the whole counsel of the Word, context and Greek grammar to discern proper biblical application. Rather it attempts to invalidate the "deacon's wife" view merely on the presupposition that since there is no qualification for the elders' wives, verse 11 must mean something else. This is a questionable method of Scripture interpretation.

Some believe verse 11 applies to the wives of both elders and deacons (i.e., Calvin). Since verse 11 starts with the "likewise" that links back to verse 8 and verse 1, there is a contextual flow for this view. Others disagree, stating the context of verse 11 only applies to deacons because verse 12 describes deacon qualifications of his marriage and family. Contextually, it would be odd to interrupt the qualification of deacons for a qualification of both deacons and elders and then go back to deacons. While it might be contextually odd it is still possible the wives of verse 11 can be applied to both elder and

---

[18] Strauch, *Paul's Vision*, 122-123.

deacon wives. It is biblical that the wives of church leaders should be quality women.

Further Grammatical and Contextual Challenges
The five views (women in general, helpers to the deacons, deaconesses, women deacons and assistants to the elders) have three additional contextual challenges.

Testing
The Greek grammar in verse 10 is specific for men to be *tested* and if found worthy *then to serve*. Verse 11, which all five views hold to as the endorsement of, and qualifications for women has no such imperative to be *tested* or to *serve*. This is a major weakness for accepting any of the five views. As illustrated above the totality of the four qualifications for women do not in totality match the ten qualifications for men. Contextually and grammatically, this keeps from attaching the imperative of verse 10 to women. If verse 11 came before verse 10 there would be an argument that verse 10 addresses the testing, worthiness and service of both men and women as deacons. So, the specific order of the verses helps to reveal contextual challenges and the significant weakness of the five views.

Authority over men
Consider further challenges for the view of women deacons. In 1 Timothy 2:12-14 Paul instructs women not to teach men or have any authority over men, but rather to remain silent. This is six verses before he addresses church leadership in 1 Timothy 3:1-13. The fact that deacons are a recognized church leadership position alone illustrates an authoritative position over men and women in the church. As church leaders, deacons have authority, and though their focus is service, they are to manage that service on behalf of Christ through elder-

appointed tasks. Acts 6 is a good example. The seven men were ordained to manage the problems of distribution to the widows. The problem was not that all widows were being neglected. There were servants distributing food, however, the distribution was not done equitably, and, as a result, division formed within the body. So, the apostles appointed the seven to manage the issue, which included managing the servants. There were an estimated 400-800 widows at that time. It is reasonable to assume there were other servants helping in the distribution of the food. The seven had authority over the other servants that were assisting. More than merely serving, deacons manage tasks from the elders with the delegated authority of Christ to make decisions and enact the necessary processes and procedures over other church servants. Paul's restriction of women not to have authority over men, by definition, would not allow women to be deacons or deaconesses as previously defined since they would be managing other church servants. This reveals a significant grammatical and contextual challenge for the view of women deacons and further weakens biblical support for the view.

Title of deacon
1 Timothy 3:1-7 provides the qualifications of an elder and uses the noun form of the word for the title. Verses 8-13 introduces the title of the office of deacon by using a specific noun form of the word in v. 8 and v. 12 where it is specifically connected to men and the verb form twice in v. 10 and v. 13. In v. 10 the men called deacon must then serve *diakoneitōsan* the verb form of the word deacon (see chapter three). In v. 13 the verb form is used again in the promise of Christ to deacons. Verse 11 does not use any form of the word deacon (noun or verb) to establish women as serving-assisting (the five views) or to

establish women with any title of deacon. This is another grammatical challenge and weakness for any of the five views.

Was Phoebe a Deacon?
Proponents of women deacons and/or deaconesses point to Romans 16:1 as one of the main arguments. The argument is based in the fact that Phoebe was a faithful servant in the church at *Cenchreae*. The idea here is that because Paul attached Phoebe's service directly to a church (*tes ekklesia*, "of the church") as a formal modifier she must have been a part of the church leadership.[19] But this argument is not iron clad.

In Romans 16, Paul recognizes a number of people who had been of service to him and others. He speaks fondly of these people and in most cases gives a quick description of their service. Paul gives the longest description to Phoebe in vv. 1-2.

> I commend to you our sister Phoebe, a servant [*diakonon*] of the church at Cenchreae, that you may welcome her in the Lord in a way worthy of the saints, and help her in whatever she may need from you, for she has been a patron of many and of myself as well. (ESV)

The NASB, ESV, KJV and other translations use the word "servant" in verse one to describe Phoebe's service to the church in Cenchreae. The NIV and NRSV translations use the word "deacon." It is obvious that Paul thinks a great deal of Phoebe; she was a faithful and dedicated servant. Paul instructs the church at Rome to "welcome her in the Lord." It is

---

[19] A. T. Robertson, *Word Pictures in the New Testament, Vol. IV: Epistles of Paul* (Grand Rapids, MI: Baker Book House 1931), 25.

probable that Phoebe was the one that delivered this letter to the church in Rome.[20]

So, was Phoebe a formal deacon of the church in *Cenchreae?*

Grammatical structure and context
The noun Paul used to describe Phoebe is *diakonos*. That word is different than the nouns Paul used when he wrote about other women servants. That alone seems odd. This is the noun Paul used in 1 Timothy 3:8, 12 and Philippians 1:1 when addressing the formal office of deacon. This noun root is the primary reason for the confusion of how to translate and understand Phoebe's position in the church. Below are several English translations of Romans 16:1:

> New International Version
> "I commend to you our sister Phoebe, a deacon of the church in Cenchreae…"
>
> New Living Translation
> "I commend to you our sister Phoebe, who is a deacon in the church in Cenchrea…"
>
> Revised Standard Version
> "I commend to you our sister Phoebe, a deaconess of the church at Cen'chre-ae…"
>
> New King James Version
> "I commend to you Phoebe our sister, who is a servant of the church in Cenchrea…"

---

[20] Gundry, *Survey*, 278.

English Standard Version
"I commend to you our sister Phoebe, a servant of the church at Cenchreae..."

New American Standard Bible
"I commend to you our sister Phoebe, who is a servant of the church which is at Cenchrea"

Christian Standard Bible
"I commend to you our sister Phoebe, who is a servant of the church in Cenchreae."

These translations refer to Phoebe as a deacon, deaconess, and servant—confusing at best. Which translation is correct? Was Phoebe a female deacon, or just one of the many believers who served in the church? Is the term "deacon" here being used as the formal title and therefore showing she had a leadership position as outlined in 1 Timothy 3?

As stated earlier, *diakonos* in Romans 16:1 is the same as 1 Timothy 3:8, 12 and Philippians 1:1. *Diakonos* is a second declension noun meaning it is either masculine or neuter in form. There is no feminine form of *diakonos* in Greek. Romans 16:1 it is masculine in form and *translated* as feminine based on context; as when attached to a woman like Phoebe. There is no firm position to take on whether or not Phoebe was a formal deacon of the church based on grammar alone. It is all within the interpretation of the context, which is why there is so much confusion and debate.

Careful attention to the context is the only way to unfold this translation mystery. When looking at grammatical structures of other passages that use *diakonos* in the context of church service it is uniformly translated "minister" or "servant." Five times *diakonos* refers to a man but is not translated as "deacon":

- Paul speaking of himself in Ephesians 3:7;
- Paul speaking of Tychicus in Ephesians 6:21;
- Paul speaking of Timothy in 1 Tim 4:6;
- Paul speaking of Epaphras in Colossians 1:7;
- Paul calls Christ a "servant" a *diakonon* in Romans 15:8, same book, one chapter earlier.

These passages use the same noun form and same grammatical structure as Romans 16:1 and are consistently translated "servant" or "minister."

As stated earlier, if Romans 16:1 is the scriptural foundation for women deacons, then there is a void in Scripture that provides the role, qualifications of the office, and how women deacons fit in the leadership structure. As was shown earlier 1 Timothy 3 is not that scriptural foundation. Deacons have delegated authority from Christ for elder-appointed tasks. Leadership and management are a major part of the deacon office, and Paul expressly stated that women are not to have authority over men (1 Tim 2:12). It is only natural that if women are to be deacons, Scripture would have provided instructions on these issues.

Timing is another contextual consideration. The book of Romans was written eight to ten years before 1 Timothy.[21] When considering if Phoebe is a formal deacon and thus a leader in her church, a part of the contextual consideration is the timing of when the office was universalized. This is the same contextual application that was made in chapter four

---

[21] Everett Harrison, *The Expositor's Bible Commentary: Romans, Vol. 10* (Grand Rapids, MI: Zondervan, 1976), 255.

when looking at Acts 6 and 1 Timothy 3 where it was determined the men of Acts 6 were technically not deacons.[22] The seven men of Acts 6 could not be deacons because the office if deacon had not yet been created. Philippians was written around AD 61 and 1 Timothy between 65-67 AD.[23] Paul addressed the church elders and deacons in Philippians. Scripture acknowledges no formal office of deacons prior to 61 AD. Thus, at the time of writing Romans in 56-57 AD there were no recognized deacons. Just as it was determined that it is inappropriate to call the seven deacons, the same contextual considerations determine that it is wrong to call Phoebe a deacon.

The translation of Romans 16:1 is difficult based on the noun Paul used. Careful study of contextual considerations shows that if women were to be deacons as part of the formal leadership structure, then there is a void in Scripture explaining their qualifications and role. However, the Word of God is not void in any area of truth, being completely sufficient in all things (2 Tim 3:14-17). Lastly, the timing of the writing of Romans is earlier than other passages that identify formal church leadership structure. For these reasons we conclude Phoebe was a faithful servant and not a deacon of her church.

Summary

God expects us to be careful and precise when handling his Word (2 Tim 2:15). In the Sermon on the Mount, Jesus said that not one little letter or jot would be overlooked. Every part

---

[22] The seven of Acts 6 initiated the office of deacon. They were servants appointed by the apostles (elders) for a delegated task. The formal office of deacon was universalized by Paul thirty years after the events of Acts 6. See chapter four.

[23] Ralph Earle, *The Expositor's Bible Commentary: 1, 2 Timothy, Vol. 11*, ed., Frank E. Gaebelein (Grand Rapids, MI: Zondervan Publishing House, 1976), 334; Robert P. Lightner, *The Bible Knowledge Commentary: Philippians*, ed. John F. Walvoord and Roy B. Zuck (Wheaton, IL: Victor Books, 1986), 647.

of Scripture is important. When we interpret his Word, we must look to pull out what is there and not filter it through our desires, church tradition, or cultural norms.

The context of 1 Timothy 3:1-13 clearly outlines the leadership structure of his church. Many commentators see the women of verse 11 as a deacon's wife, given the Greek grammatical structure and contextual considerations. Verses 8-10 are necessary character qualifications of the deacon. Verse 11 provides the necessary qualifications of a deacon's wife, and verse 12 provides qualifications of his marriage and family life.

However, other interpreters see the women in verse 11 in one of the following five views:

1. Any female servant

2. Assistants to male deacons

3. Assistants to elders

4. Deaconesses

5. Female deacons equal in all ways to male deacons

After working through grammatical and contextual considerations it was determined these are not proper interpretations. There is greater support to the view that verse 11 describes qualifications for a deacon's wife.

Phoebe was a tremendous servant to her home church in Cenchreae, to Paul, and probably to the church in Rome during her stay. The grammar of Romans 16:1, like that of 1 Timothy 3:11, does not support her being a part of the formal leadership of the church in Cenchreae, which is further supported by Paul's instruction in 2 Timothy 2:12 that women are not the have authority over men. Furthermore, contextual considerations of other passages that use *diakonos* and the timing of the writing of Romans show that Phoebe was not part of formal leadership since the office of deacon was not yet fully established. Likely Phoebe carried Paul's letter to the Romans, and though that was an official task, she was not an official leader of the Cenchreae church.[24]

Christ has gifted all his believers to serve his church. As a community, we are to serve each other all for the glory of God. It is not ours to add to or change the structure of leadership of his church, and we must be careful to not allow outside influences of tradition, secular culture, or personal desires to cloud our interpretation of his Word.

---

[24] Benjamin Merkle, "The Authority of Deacons in Pauline Churches," *Journal of the Evangelical Theological Society*, Scottsdale, AZ, vol. 64, 309.

Jesus said, "**I will build my church** and the gates of hell shall not prevail against it."
Matthew 16:18

Apostle Paul said, "**Christ is the head of the church**, his body, and is himself its Savior."
Ephesians 5:23

9

Conclusion

Matthew 16:18 and Ephesians 5:23 make it clear that Christ is the head of the church, and he will grow his church globally and locally at his will, in his timing, and Satan will never prevail against it. However, many do not incorporate these two verses when considering the leadership structure of their local church. These verses directly address church leadership, establishing Christ as the head of the church. His divine instructions set the direction and standards by which the local church is to operate. Christ demands that we handle his Word with precision. Eve abandoned God's Word for her own reasoning, and all of humanity was plunged into ruin (Gen 3:1-6). Christ perfectly fought off Satan in the wilderness through precise understanding and use of the Scriptures (Matt 4:1-11). It is all important. When we interpret his Word, we must look to apply what is there and not filter it through our desires, church tradition, cultural norms, or anything else.

Through special revelation given to the apostles, Christ established a specific leadership structure for his churches. It is not a mystery. It includes **two offices** each with a plurality of men: elders and deacons (1 Tim 3:1-13). There are **two**

directives: elders are to shepherd the flock of God (1 Pet 5:1-2); deacons are to serve (1 Tim 3:10). There is **one purpose:** for the Word of God to be proclaimed and to increase the number of believers (Acts 6:7).

Throughout 2,000 years of church history, man has moved away from the simple and elegant church leadership structure established by Christ. Originating from church traditions, denominational practices, and man introducing his own views into his interpretation of Scripture, there are five major church structures vying for prominence today with few churches following the elder-shepherding model as universalized by Paul in 1 Timothy 3:1-13.

In Matthew 23 and Luke 11 Jesus reached one of his most indignant moments when addressing the first-century religious leaders, the scribes and Pharisees, who for centuries foisted man-made laws on to the Mosaic Law, thereby making man's laws equal to God's law. This was religious legalism at its worst. And Just as the Pharisees did over 2,000 years ago, these church structures outside of Christ's prescribed structure in 1 Timothy 3 have brought confusion, division and even destructive practices to today's churches. These deviant church models diminish Scripture because they are outside the boundary of Christ's command in 1 Timothy 3. They diminish God's Word by watering down Paul's instructions or by bringing additional elements to church structure that are outside of Scripture.

These wayward structures have introduced harmful teachings, including the following:

- Deacons are to be shepherds
- Extra-biblical qualifications
- Women in formal church leadership

CONCLUSION

- Congregational overreach in the selection process

The proper exegesis of Scripture defines the role of deacons to be serving and managing as appointed by local elders on behalf of Christ for the church body to the glory of God. Because Scripture is sufficient, adding qualifications undermines the sufficiency of the Word and tends toward legalism. The service of women is essential to the body, but they are not to be in positions of headship, including the formal offices of the church. Congregations are to be involved in the selection of its leaders, but it is the elders' responsibility to appoint men to leadership as well as to provide direction for the body's involvement.

Two Offices

The office of elder has headship and is a priority within the church. In Paul's missionary journeys, his first priority was to establish elders (Acts 14:23). He also instructed Titus to do the same (Titus 1:5). Elders are the shepherds, and like the apostles in Acts 6, it is through the elders that areas of service are identified for deacons to serve.[1] Nowhere in the New Testament do we see deacons established prior to elders. Christ's leadership model for the church is to first establish elders, the spiritual leaders who preach, teach, pray, and guide God's people. Then in time, the elders appoint deacons to serve when service needs a rise, as modeled in Acts 6.

It is common to think that because elders have headship and priority the office of elder is elevated above deacon in importance. That would not be a proper biblical perspective. Elders and deacons are equally important to the church.

---

[1] See chapter four for an explanation of how the seven men of Acts 6 initiated what later became the formal office of deacons (1 Tim 3:8-13).

Nowhere in Scripture is one office elevated in its importance over the other. Both offices have crucial duties to the church. Both have specific roles for the church to properly function. A functioning church with elders and no deacons puts a strain on elders to be meeting the church body's spiritual needs (Acts 6:2) because they are getting distracted with other time-consuming necessities. A functioning church with deacons and no elders has no shepherds to care for the flock. A healthy church with Christ-centered leadership has both elders and deacons, equally important to each other and the body, which bring the harmony of Acts 6:7.

Two Directives
Each office has a primary directive. The elders' directive is the ministry of the Word. In the last chapter of John's Gospel, Christ looks at Peter and tells him, "feed My lambs," "tend My sheep," and "feed My sheep" (John 21:15-17). The directive for elders is to be the under-shepherds for Christ.

The deacons' primary directive is service (1 Tim 3:10). Deacons are to serve the church by fulfilling important and critical service items identified by the elders. This was first seen in Acts 6:1-3. The early church in Jerusalem had a serious problem with daily food distribution to the widows. The apostles established a specific process to identify men to attend to the needs of the widows. Acts 6 initiated what Paul would later universalize into the formal office of deacon. These men became the first recognized servants of Christ's church. Their service provided proper care for widows, calmed issues between other people within the church, and allowed the apostles to keep their attention focused on the ministry of the Word. The widows were served. The apostles maintained their focus, and it brought order and stability to the problem. The church at large was well served. This is the model of deacon service. Paul finalized the office in 1 Timothy 3, expanding the role of deacons beyond waiting tables to include any service assigned by the elders.

One Purpose

Acts 6 initiated the office of deacon and models the proper structure between the offices Christ intends for his leaders. Acts 6:2-4, 6 reads:

> And the twelve summoned the full number of the disciples and said, "It is not right that we should give up preaching the word of God to serve tables. **Therefore, brothers, pick out** from among you seven men of good repute, full of the Spirit and of wisdom, **whom we will appoint to this duty**. But we will devote ourselves to prayer and to the ministry of the word"…These (the seven) they set before the apostles, and they prayed and laid their hands on them.

When the apostles saw the problem with service to the widows, they did the following:

1. Diagnosed the problem

2. Took initiative

3. Communicated the purpose, plan and process to the community

4. Examined the seven

5. Ordained the seven

The apostles saw the need, oversaw the process of selection, ordained and assigned the service task. These seven men answered the need, and the newly appointed servants served the church. Two offices working together as designed by Christ to serve his Bride, the Church. Two offices, each with directives, focused on one purpose: being Christ's servant-leaders to love and serve the church body. When done properly Acts 6:7 is the result: "and the word of God continued to increase, and the number of the disciples multiplied greatly."

Plurality is Christ's Model

> This is why I left you in Crete, so that you might put what remained into order, and appoint **elders** in every town as I directed you (Titus 1:5).

The first century Jewish people had no problem with a plurality in leadership. Plurality of leaders has always been God's model since the Exodus of Israel from Egypt. Moses and Aaron established multiple leaders as Jethro counseled (Exod 18:17-26). Christ trained a plurality of apostles who were the leaders of the early church. Those apostles initiated the office of deacon with a plurality of men. The apostles could have chosen one person—it was a singular task, after all—and that person could have then managed a group of people to accomplish said task. But the apostles followed the plurality model God had always used either by historical standards or by divine inspiration when establishing the ordained servants in Acts 6. Paul opened the letter to the Philippians recognizing both elders and deacons, a plurality of men in both offices of a church he established.

The church's theological structure establishes the spiritual headship of the church. The church also has an operational structure that establishes how leadership interacts with the servants of the church.

A commonly asked question: Is it wrong to attend a church where deacons serve in the role of elders? Scripture does not say it is sinful to attend a church with a bad leadership structure. However, one should not be surprised if the leadership is dysfunctional, or if their teaching on leadership is misguided. Regardless of leadership, we are all called to be Bereans, to examine Scripture (Acts 17:11) and to be discerning in all things:

> For God is my witness, how I yearn for you all with the affection of Christ Jesus. And it is my prayer that your love may abound more and more, with knowledge and all discernment, so that you may approve what is excellent, and so be pure and blameless for the day of Christ (Phil 1:8-10).

Just as the world needs a gospel revival, the church needs a revival in leadership structure established by Christ, particularly in what the Bible has to say about the misunderstood office of deacon.

"Therefore, be careful how you walk, not as unwise men but as wise."
Ephesians 5:15

Appendix 1
Best Practices

With over 2,000 years of church history, there are examples of bad, good, better, and best practices for church leadership structure. These include deacon qualifications, the nomination process for deacons, selection process, the scope of a deacon's ministry, the length of term of office, and more. This chapter will reveal bad practices that either go outside Scripture, or foist man's preferences onto Scripture, or are improperly divisive and hurtful to the body in each of these areas. We will also identify some best practices that follow Scripture and promote harmony in the body of Christ.

Leadership Structure: Deacon Shepherds and Deacon Boards

Churches that use the Local-Democratic leadership structure typically blur the line between elders and deacons, having deacons provide headship and spiritual ministry to the body.[1] They usually have a single pastor (elder) and multiple deacons who are chosen with minimal input from the pastor. Frequently, these churches use a "corporate-like" leadership

---

[1] "Note the similarity of the spiritual qualifications that are established for the pastor and for the deacons in 1 Timothy 3. These qualifications speak of the kind of person that both leaders are 'to be.' They are to be spiritual men on a spiritual mission. The Scriptures do not speak of the exact work that either pastor or deacons are to do." Howard B. Foshee, *Now That You're a Deacon* (Nashville, TN: B&H Publishing Group, 1975), 25.

structure with a chairman, a board, and many committees. The chairman's job can range from overseeing the general direction of the deacon Family Plan;[2] being the right-hand man of the pastor; presiding over deacon meetings; overseeing the church program; being the receiver of all complaints.[3] However, the most alarming element of these churches is the view that the congregation has the last word by voting —some level of majority rules on critical issues; hiring/firing a lead pastor; adding/deleting elders and deacons; budget; church discipline; and more.

The above structure is used by many Baptist churches and often creates leadership challenges.[4] This flawed structure starts with having a single pastor. Paul's instructions are clear that a local church is to have multiple elders (Acts 14:23; Titus 1:5). God's plan for using multiple men in leadership began with Israel in the Old Testament (Num 11:16) and continued in the New Testament with the church. Christ did not design his church to have a single man be the spiritual leader over his flock. Further, Christ did not design the church to have both tiers of the leadership (elders/deacons) lead the flock spiritually. It is common for deacons to misunderstand their role in churches with this type of structure. Many deacons believe that they comprise a second group of overseer-elders

---

[2] "The deacon Family Plan. This is a pattern of organization designed to reach every family in the church by regular visitation in homes. Church families are grouped in some systematic ways and assigned to deacons who serve as shepherds of their smaller flock. Each deacon is responsible for the pastoral care of twelve to fifteen families." Foshee, *Now That You're a Deacon*, 17.

[3] Robert Naylor, *The Baptist Deacon* (Nashville, TN: Broadman and Holman Publishers, 1955), 65.

[4] "Tension between pastor and deacons is not uncommon in churches. Often this results in open warfare, which then cripples the influence and work of such churches. Some pastors feel that they cannot work through their deacons. They have been heard to say, 'I know what I will do. If my deacons will not go along with me, I will take it to the church and let the congregation decide.'" Naylor, *The Baptist Deacon*, 3.

or that they are to provide checks and balances to the elders.[5] This is clearly not how Christ has structured his church.

First Timothy 3 gives elders freedom in their oversight of the church, but this freedom does not include changing the leadership structure. The structure was established by Christ. It is simple and elegant and not to be changed or altered in any way.

Best practice
Of the five listed leadership structures identified in chapter two, "elder shepherding" is the only model that follows a proper interpretation of 1 Timothy 3:1-13. Christ provided a detailed and specific leadership structure with elders as the spiritual leaders of the church and deacons to serve and manage others in delegated tasks from the elders. Elders have authority in their church, and they are not to abdicate their spiritual headship to anyone. In Acts 15, Paul, Barnabas, and several others were appointed to go to Jerusalem and discuss a very serious spiritual issue about whether new Gentile believers had to be circumcised. It leaves one to wonder why "several others" were appointed to go if they were not elders. If elders are not to abdicate their spiritual oversight, then why are non-elders appointed to go with Paul and Barnabas? Nevertheless, when it came time to have the discussion, only the apostles and elders of Jerusalem were involved (15:6, 12). There was an assembly that listened, but they did not take part in the debate. The elders are the church leaders, and all ministries fall under their authority. Christ did not create a head elder or chairman that has any more authority or power over the others. Christ did not intend for deacons to have spiritual authority over the

---

[5] Alexander Strauch, *Paul's Vision for the Deacons* (Littleton, CO: Lewis and Roth Publishers, 2017), 80.

flock. Operating outside the structure created by Christ invites misapplication of the Bible, poor thinking, poor modeling, divisiveness, and failed leadership.

Below is a chart of church theological structure illustrating Christ as the Head of the Church with the Word as its foundation with local church leadership structure within the universal Church

Theological Structure

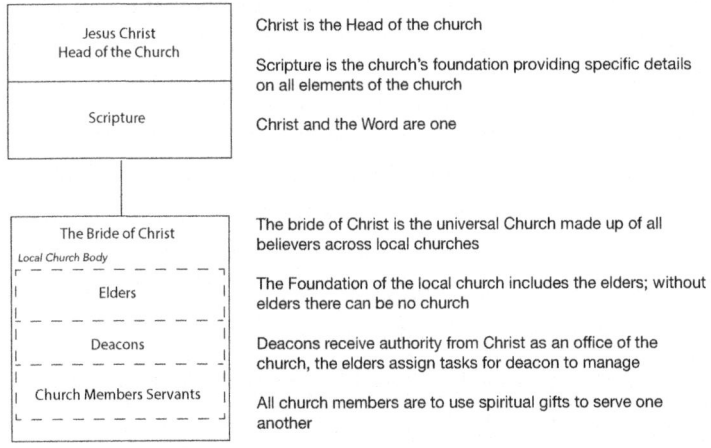

So how does the theological structure work out in every day practical ministry? Below is a chart that illustrates the operational workings of the above chart detailing the theological structure.

In our church, elders oversee every ministry. Deacons are assigned areas to serve and manage others in the ministry on behalf of and working with the elders to update them and get input from them as needed. As an example, our church is located on a busy street next to a public park. Our security ministry makes sure the campus is secure by walking the campus before and during Sunday services. They also oversee transitions for children to go to children's church and other events. The campus security ministry is managed by one of our deacons who coordinates all details of the ministry with other saints and reports to the elder who is the overseer. It is common for the deacon to work with the elder on issues within ministry and seek the elder's input.

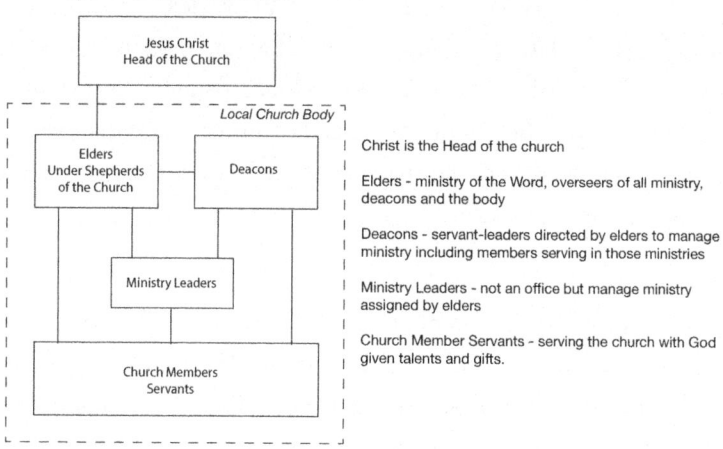

There are other ministry leaders in the church who are not deacons but who work directly with the elders. The nursery ministry is a good example. We have two ladies that manage the nursery ministry and all of its moving parts, coordinating volunteers, establishing curriculum, getting supplies and more. These ladies have been given freedom in their management, but they regularly coordinate with the elder who oversees the ministry.

This structure established by Christ keeps the elders informed of all ministries while allowing the body to serve one another as outlined in Scripture. The elders can hear and see first-hand ministries that are growing. They are involved to help give insight and see how best to support lay leaders.

Qualifications

Many authors state that a man needs to desire the position of deacon, but do not recognize "desire" as a specific qualification or address how it should be examined.[6] Chapter five addressed the qualifications of deacons. The context of a "trustworthy saying" links the qualification of "aspiring" to the office of deacon.

Aspiring to the office of elder or deacon is just as important as all other qualifications. If a man does not properly aspire to the office, he should not be installed as a church leader. A man who is not convinced of his calling will not make a good leader. "Aspiring to the office" is equal to any other qualification in 1 Timothy 3:8-12.

Best practice

It's been my experience that men who are servants are focused on meeting the service needs of the church and usually do not like to be out front or upheld as leaders. They like being behind the scenes serving with their God-given talents. When men of this nature are asked if they "aspire," it is not uncommon for them to struggle in their initial response. They do not consider their service to be worthy of leadership and are apprehensive to be considered a leader. It is common for a deacon candidate to need time to consider the weight of all qualifications and have multiple conversations with the elders, giving time for God to work on the heart of the deacon candidate. In the end,

---

[6] "Unless a man can make a spiritual contribution to leadership in the body, he has no reason for being elected as a deacon. As previously mentioned, the call of a deacons comes initially from the church, each man in the church should be ready to respond to the call of the church. As he considers the responsibilities of the office, each man must determine before God if He would have him serve in this capacity. The call of the church alone is not sufficient to make a man a good deacon. His own response and dedication before God will determine his effectiveness in the office...Too many men elected to the office revel in the honor placed upon them and never submit themselves to the service to which they are called." J.D. O'Donnell, *Handbook for Deacons* (Nashville, TN: Randall House Publications, 1973), 40-41.

they have to affirm God's call for themselves to be a leader in the church and meet all qualifications of the position.

This qualification of aspiring to the office and the "being tested" discussed in chapter five are two elements of choosing a deacon that are often overlooked. Over the years I have met men that meet the other qualifications listed in vv. 8-12, but they either did not have any desire for the office, or they were not properly tested prior to becoming a deacon. It is not surprising these men were not good deacons.

> **Deacon Qualifications of 1 Timothy 3:8-12**
>
> - Aspire to the office
> - Dignified
> - Not double-tongued
> - Not addicted to much wine
> - Not greedy for dishonest gain
> - Hold the mystery of the faith with a clear conscience
> - Examined and found blameless
> - His wife is dignified, not a slanderer, sober-minded and faithful in all things
> - Husband of one wife
> - Manages their children and their own households well

Church-added qualifications

There are many who believe the qualifications of Scripture are not adequate, and, as a result, suggest further qualifications are needed. This blatantly undermines the doctrine of biblical sufficiency. Henry Webb suggests in his book, *Deacons*, the following added qualifications for deacon candidates: a minimum age; to be a church member for an established period of time; attendance across church functions; being a tither, giving a minimum of ten percent of one's income.[7]

As previously discussed, the elders are given much authority in 1 Timothy 3. Adding qualifications to the church's

---

[7] Henry Webb, *Deacons: Servant Models in the Church* (Nashville, TN: B&H Publishing Group, 2001), 3-4.

leadership structure established by Christ does not fall within that sphere of authority. If these "added qualifications" were within the definition of the listed qualifications of 1 Timothy 3:8-12, or if they were a part of the examination process listed in verse 10, then they would be appropriate and helpful. But they are not, and because of this, implementing them undermines the authority of the Word, and sets a precedent for adding more man-based qualifications, which ultimately hurts the body. Adding these types of qualifications leads to wrong teaching, a poor evaluation process, and missing truly qualified candidates.

In his book, *The Baptist Deacon*, Robert Naylor says deacons need to be businessmen. He quotes from the King James Version of Acts 6:3, where the Apostles give three qualifications for the seven, "Wherefore, brethren, look ye out among you seven men of honest report, full of the Holy Ghost and wisdom, whom we may appoint over this business."[8] Naylor completely misses the interpretation, using "appoint over this business" to justify that deacons should be businessman. There are three major problems with this view. First, Naylor asserts the task the seven are being appointed to as qualification for the office of deacon. This creates a fourth qualification in Acts 6 that is not supported from the passage itself nor its context. Second, Naylor is dependent upon the KJV, which is the only major version that translates the Greek word χρείας as "business" (Acts 6:3). This is best translated as "need," "task," or "duty" and is translated accordingly in the

---

[8] "The deacons should have certain secular qualifications. These receive minor treatment in the Scriptures; but because of the things they were to do it was taken for granted that they would represent the best of human leadership. The instruction in the selection of the seven was that they should be men who could be appointed 'over this business' (v. 3 KJV). It is very plain that a new rank of ministerial orders was not being created but that secular responsibilities were being distributed. If too much is not made of the modern meaning of the term it is safe to say that these seven were businessmen." Naylor, *The Baptist Deacon*, 20.

other major translations. Wrong interpretation leads to misapplication that leads to improper men in leadership roles, causing harm to the church body. Third, as established in chapter four, the men of Acts 6 are not deacons. Though the qualification of Acts 6 and 1 Timothy 3 mirror each other, the fullness of deacon qualifications for the New Testament church come from Paul when he universalized the office in 1 Timothy 3.

Webb and Naylor use man-based, extra-biblical qualifications. It is this type of wrong thinking that led to the bad practices beginning in the second century, which are still going on today. Beware man's wisdom that adds to God's qualifications for his leaders. They create wrong thinking. More importantly, they create an environment of missing potentially good candidates.

Best practice
Do not add qualifications beyond that of Scripture (1 Cor 4:6). It is bad practice to teach a body of believers to follow the instructions of Scripture alone but at the same time go beyond Scripture in practice by creating superfluous qualifications for a deacon. Such requirements are legalistic because they go beyond the clear mandates of God's Word. Vet each deacon candidate through the qualifications of 1 Timothy 3, searching for the man of integrity and character that God has for your church.

In our church we have had deacons whose occupations include truck driver, hospital technician, database designer, construction contractor, software developer, city government employee, engineer, as well as businessman. If we added the qualification that they were to be businessmen, we would have overlooked over half of our deacons.

The Nomination Process

Scripture does not prescribe a particular nomination process. As we saw in Acts 6, the apostles instructed the congregation to select (nominate) seven men for the apostles to then examine, ordain, and appoint to the task. As was concluded in chapter four, Acts 6 introduced the use of representative government. But the process used there is not a mandatory model; local elders have the authority to establish how the congregation will affirm prospective leaders (1 Tim 3:10). Across the landscape of today's churches, some nomination processes are held in open with the whole church body. Some are private processes. Some have nomination committees.[9] Some involve elders in the nomination process; many do not. Regardless of the nomination process used, Paul required all deacon candidates to be examined (by the church and elders) and ultimately appointed to tasks and ordained by the elders (1 Tim 3:10). Nowhere does Scripture call for the local church members to select its leaders without the examination by the elders.

A good example of *wrong thinking* followed by *poor implementation* comes from O'Donnell in his book, *Handbook for Deacons*. O'Donnell proclaims that the congregation is to appoint deacons exclusive of elder approval.[10] This wrong thinking does not align with what we learned in chapter four about Acts 6 and 1 Timothy 3. O'Donnell further states that deacons are to be spiritual leaders—this is poor implementation considering the teaching we see in 1 Timothy 3 that designates on elders to be the local church's spiritual leaders. Naylor and O'Donnell both misinterpret the Acts 6

---

[9] Webb, *Deacons*, 5.
[10] O'Donnell, *Handbook*, 40-41.

model, asserting that final deacon selection must be made through democratic congregational choice.[11]

A deacon candidate should consider his motives and desire regarding the position as discussed in chapter five. However, requiring that a deacon must be chosen by the congregation, eliminating the approval process of the elders, violates Scripture.

Paul calls for elders to appoint deacons and gives elders autonomy in how to involve the church in deacon selection. Naylor and Webb have it upside down. Paul did not allow for the congregation to take over the process of selecting men without using biblical qualifications, without being tested as a servant, and without being examined by elders. O'Donnell's process is flawed and results in the outcome he predicted in that men do not serve properly.

Best practice

Elders must determine when and where deacons are needed. This practice is modeled in Acts 6 where the apostles decided the best way to address the issue of the widows was to find worthy men to delegate the task. When elders determine that deacon(s) are needed for certain tasks, Scripture demands they look to men who are gifted in service with a history of service to examine (1 Tim 3:10).

Elders are to know their sheep (John 21:15-17). They should know potential candidates. Before involving the body, the elders should examine the potential candidates to determine if they aspire to the office and meet the qualifications. Once the elders are convinced a man meets the qualifications of 1 Timothy 3, and properly aspires to the office, it is then time to involve the congregation. Several

---

[11] Naylor, *The Baptist Deacon*, 35.

authors are concerned that nomination from the elders alone could create favoritism or one-sided leadership. Or, if the candidate does not make a good deacon, it would reflect negatively on the elder(s) who nominated them.[12] This is a legitimate concern if a church has unqualified elders, or elders who ignore the biblical process. This is an illegitimate objection if the elders truly know their people and are looking for and evaluating men to become their next deacons, and if they are following the process laid out in the Bible. For churches who have only a single pastor, the concern of favoritism can be legitimate. This is one of many reasons Paul instructs churches to have multiple elders.

In our church, candidates are usually put forward by one of the elders. It is most common for a vocational elder (full-time pastor) to nominate the candidate as they tend to work more directly with the congregation, but a nomination can come from any elder. Members can also put forward a candidate by initiating a discussion with an elder.

The elders perform an initial review of the candidate's past service discussing their quality of service, how they work with others in their area(s) of service, how they work with the elders, and the potential deacon's qualifications in light of 1 Timothy 3. Once the elders agree on a man to examine more deeply, the elder over deacons meets with the candidate.

There are typically two to three meetings to review their service, qualifications, and aspiration to the office. Depending on how those discussions go, additional meetings are set, including the candidate meeting with other current deacons. The last meeting(s) is/are with the deacon candidate and his wife (if married) to review the qualifications of a deacon's wife

---

[12] O'Donnell, *Handbook*, 38.

in verse 11, and get her perspective about her husband in the role of deacon. We also talk about the promise of verse 13, the challenge of church leadership and the attacks of Satan on church leaders. If any time during those meetings it is determined the man does not aspire to the office, has improper motivations, or seems to not be qualified, then the nomination process is halted. The elders then decide whether to search for another candidate or wait.

If during the above nomination process a candidate is found lacking in qualifications, that does not remove him from future consideration. In Acts 15:36-40 Paul found John Mark lacking and did not want him to join the next missionary journey. Barnabas believed John Mark had matured and wanted him to come along. A resolution could not be established, and Paul and Barnabas split with Barnabas taking John Mark to Cyprus and Paul taking Silas on the next missionary journey. In 2 Timothy 4:11, later in his life and ministry, Paul asks for John Mark, "for he is very useful to me for ministry." People grow and mature in Christ as Christ sanctifies us for his purpose (1 Thess 5:23). Just because a man is not qualified for the office today does not mean he should not be considered again in the future.

Once the elders agree that the candidate is qualified and ready, he is put forward to the congregation to be affirmed or rejected.

Congregational Selection

It is proper for congregations to participate in selecting their leaders. This is seen in Acts 6 and supported in 1 Timothy 3. Voting on deacon candidates is a common practice. However, most authors do not suggest parameters or best practices for the voting. What should the voting standard be to accept a candidate? Simple majority? Super majority? Unanimous consent? Can a single "no vote" of a church of 1,000 people tank a candidate? The Bible does not give the details on how the seven were chosen in Acts 6.[13] Were there nominations of more than seven men and then reduced to seven? Any public debate? Verbal or written votes? We do not know. The elders of a local church need to involve and hear from the congregation on the selection of new elders and deacons. While a public vote is not wrong, there are some inherent problems:

- A public vote usually means there has been public discussion that can lead to improper talk, gossip, and even open accusations of sin.

- A public vote can involve politicking for or against a candidate, with private discussions that are based on inappropriate areas of service or emphasizing inappropriate attributes.

- If there is a vote, then usually that means there is a choice between multiple candidates. If all candidates are biblically qualified, how is a man chosen? Singular issues like popularity, or being a long-time member, or having been nominated multiple times, or being a good family man, or

---

[13] See chapter four. In Acts 6, the formal office of deacon had not yet been established, so the seven appointed by the Apostles were not technically deacons. However, as discussed in chapter four, the qualifications established by the Apostles were extraordinarily similar to the qualification Paul universalized in 1 Timothy 3. The assigned task of serving widows for the Seven in Acts 6 is similar to the general task of service for deacons in 1 Timothy 3. The Seven in Acts 6 initiated the office of deacon that was universalized by Paul thirty years later in 1 Timothy 3. The Apostles in Acts 6 initiated the role, using the community of believers to select the Seven. This was different than how leaders were chosen in the Old Testament. Following Scripture and Acts 6. the local church congregation is to be involved in the selection of its leaders as directed by its elders.

Appendix 1: Best Practices

unbiblical reasons like being a good businessman can come into play.
- Nominees that have been brought up multiple times and not affirmed can be hurt and feel rejected by both leaders and the congregation.

What is the optimal procedure by which the elders can avoid these issues and still involve the church body in the selection process?

Best practice
Deacons are appointed to tasks by elders and operate through elder-delegated authority (1 Tim 3:10). So, it follows that the elders select the man to examine their past service and analyze him through the filter of biblical qualifications (1 Tim 3:8-12). When the elders believe they have found a qualified candidate, it is time to involve the congregation.

In our church, we do not examine multiple men simultaneously to find a single candidate. We do not bring to the congregation multiple candidates asking them to select one. We believe a competitive selection process can be harmful and divisive.

Once the elders have agreed on a candidate, the process of involving our members begins with our lead pastor sending an email to our members. That email gives a high-level description of the candidate's background, results of the elders' examination, request for prayer as well as input, and both endorsements for and concerns about the candidate. We give our church members three weeks to think, pray, and connect with the elders with endorsements or concerns. Endorsements are forwarded to the elders. This helps the elders see confirmation from the body. Concerns are taken very seriously. A single negative response can bring an end to a candidate's consideration. In congregations that have voting, sometimes there can be multiple people with concerns, however, if they are in the minority, they are then overruled and the deacon is installed—sometimes to the peril of the church.

Our lead pastor connects with members that have concerns and vets out the issue. All feedback from members about the candidate is shared with the deacon candidate, whether positive or negative. If there is negative feedback or a concern is raised, that member must talk privately with the candidate about it. If there is unrepentant sin, then we will follow Matthew 18:15-17 to address the sin and restore any broken relationships. If our member has qualification concerns, our lead pastor will hear out the concern and take the appropriate action. The member must have had direct interaction with the candidate on the concern. We do not allow members to discuss a concern on behalf of others or from rumor. Sometimes a concern comes from an unresolved issue(s) that is not based in sin. We then have the member and candidate meet to see if the issue can be resolved.

Once concerns are properly investigated, the information is shared with all the elders to make a final determination on the candidate. Men are not perfect. We don't look for perfect men. We look for men of character and integrity that properly address and handle concerns that have been raised. Legitimate issues raised by members must have had proper resolution or the candidate would not be moved forward. Once affirmed by the membership and the elders are confident of God's calling, they will lay hands on the candidate on a special Sunday morning worship, ordaining him into service (Acts 6:6).

APPENDIX 1: BEST PRACTICES

Ministry of a Deacon

There are numerous views of what a deacon's ministry entails. Below I address four of the more disputed areas: (1) Is a deacon a spiritual leader or one who focuses on service? (2) Who chooses how and where a deacon will service? (3) What is the proper scope of ministries for a deacon? (4) How long should the term of a deacon be?

Spiritual-leader or service-leader

Throughout the book, we have laid the foundation that deacons work in areas of service overseen by the elders on behalf of Christ for the body to the glory of God. We have noted the perplexity that can surround this church office, including confusion from long-standing deacons[14] to newly-elected ones who are unsure of their responsibilities or addled about how to perform them.[15]

This confusion is based in a foundational misinterpretation of Scripture that begins with bad leadership structures (discussed earlier in this chapter) flowing down to the misapplication of deacon duties. For example, Foshee proclaims deacons to be spiritual leaders and one of their primary areas of service is the "deacon Family Ministry Plan," where they are shepherds to 12-15 families.[16] Foshee believes pastors and deacons are co-leaders in the spiritual ministry to

---

[14] "In many places the office and service of deacons is ill-defined and little understood. The average Baptist would have the haziest kind of idea about what a deacon ought to do...I was asked to spend Saturday evening with the deacons discussing their function and service. Late in the discussion one man said, 'say, if I had known all this before I became a deacon I wouldn't be one.'" Naylor, *The Baptist Deacon*, 2.

[15] Harold Nichols, *The Work of the Deacon & Deaconess* (Valley Forge, PA: Judson Press, 2014), 103.

[16] "One channel of deacon service is the deacon Family Ministry Plan. This is a pattern of organizational designed to reach every family in the church by regular visitation in homes. Church families are grouped in some systematic ways and assigned to deacons who serve as shepherds of their small flock. Each deacon is responsible for the pastoral care of the twelve to fifteen families." Foshee, *Now That You're a Deacon*, 17.

the body and that Scripture does not outline exact roles for pastors and deacons.[17] Webb agrees with Foshee, believing each deacon is to directly minister to 10-15 families.[18]

The old saying "it starts from the top" is true in this case. Poor structure leads to poorly defined roles that inevitably results in poor implementation, which in the church's case affects ministry and the body.

Who chooses how and where a deacon will serve

Foshee believes deacons are to be spiritual leaders. He also believes that after a man has been selected to be a deacon, then he needs to determine how to apply his gifts and how to serve.[19] This is a common practice in many churches where men are not selected based on their past service in the church or biblical qualifications, but rather from their social or business standing. These men are usually selected because they are popular, charismatic, successful in business, or natural leaders. We saw this earlier in this chapter when discussing churches who add their own qualifications, such as requiring deacons to be businessmen. Naylor addressed this situation, explaining that it is common for the ministry of a deacon to be poorly defined or misunderstood even by the men holding the

---

[17] "Note the similarity of the spiritual qualifications that are established for the pastor and for the deacons in 1 Timothy 3. These qualifications speak of the kind of person that both leaders are 'to be.' They are to be spiritual men on a spiritual mission. The scriptures do not speak of the exact work that either pastor or deacons are to do. Rather, God emphasized what these co-leaders in ministry are to be. Each should always be in the process of becoming." Foshee, *Now That You're a Deacon*, 25.

[18] Webb, *Deacons*, 85.

[19] "Now that you are a deacon, give thought to your special gifts or talents. What gifts do you bring for service as a deacon? What kind of different gifts are there? Gifts are legion. Have you ever tried to list the gifts God gave you? Do you have special talent for teaching, building fellowship, shepherding, or caring, witnessing, reconciliation, stewardship, administration, prayer, speaking or preaching? This is just the beginning, for God gives many talents. Determine to find out your strengths so that you can give them in service as a deacon." Foshee, *Now That You're a Deacon*, 41.

office.[20] Oddly enough though, Naylor is also one who claims that deacons are to help in areas of spiritual headship that fall into the role of elders, which adds to the confusion.

These are not bad churches or bad men. These views come from a flawed selection process and poor teaching on leadership. The Apostle Paul had five sayings that he taught his congregations. One was on leadership. That explains how important proper leadership was to Paul.

Best practice

Paul defined the selection process in 1 Timothy 3:10. A deacon candidate is to be tested first, meaning his past service is examined through the lens of the qualifications and how he works with other servants and the elders. When candidates are viewed from their past service, then the candidate, the elders, and the church know the candidate's gifts and talents, which allows them to properly evaluate them and enables them to decide where they can best serve the congregation.

In Acts 6, the apostles appointed the task to the seven. In 1 Timothy 3, Paul has the elders assign tasks. The deacon does not choose his task. They are assigned and overseen by the elders. In our church, when the elders put forward a new deacon candidate that is approved by the congregation, the new deacon will typically continue working in the area(s) he was already serving, where he is gifted. Over time the elders may need to re-task the deacon into other areas of need as things change in the body.

---

[20] "In many places the office and service of deacons is ill defined and little understood. The average Baptist would have the haziest kind of idea about what a deacon ought to do. What does the office of deacon mean to the church? What is the responsibility of the deacon? What is his function?...I was asked to spend Saturday evening with the deacons discussing their function and service...late in the discussion one man said, 'say, if I had known all this before I became a deacon I wouldn't be one.'" Naylor, *The Baptist Deacon*, 2.

One of our deacons has had his area of responsibility changed multiple times. Initially, he was the church "IT guy" helping to manage the computers and other office technology. Later he helped manage facilities. Later still, he was asked to manage the ushers and greeters. Some of our other deacons have remained in one area of service for many years. Overall, it is the duty of the elders to assign deacons tasks best suited for their God-given gifts and abilities for the glory of God and benefit of the body.

Scope of Ministries for Deacons
One of the most debated issues today is defining the scope of a deacon's service. Many believe the scope is to be based in the mercy ministry of the seven in Acts, demonstrating the love of Christ by providing for the poor and afflicted.[21] Most who hold to this position see the seven as the first deacons, contending that only in recent church history has this been questioned.[22] Early church Reformers, including Luther and Calvin, removed the liturgical functions typically assigned to deacons by the Catholic Church, believing they should follow the model of Acts 6.[23] Those coming from this view see Acts 6 as the proper deacon model as established by the apostles.

The problem with this view is that the men in Acts 6 only initiated the office of deacon; the office was universalized thirty years later in 1 Timothy 3. Paul expands the role of deacons to more than table-servers. Elders have the authority to assign deacons to any task, in keeping with what the apostles

---

[21] Cornelis Van Dam, *The Deacon: Biblical Foundations for Today's Ministry of Mercy* (Grand Rapids, MI: Reformation Heritage Books, 2016), xi.
[22] Francis Martin and Thomas Oden, *Acts: Ancient Christian Commentary on Scripture – New Testament Volume 5* (Downers Grove, IL: InterVaristy Press, 2006), 70-71.
[23] Jeannine Olson, *Deacon and Deaconesses Through the Centuries* (St. Louis, MO: Concordia Publishing House, 2005), 118-129.

Appendix 1: Best Practices

did in Acts 6.[24] A comprehensive view of Scripture must include both passages with an understanding of the broader scope and universalized office of 1 Timothy 3.

Best practice

The command by Paul in 1 Timothy 3:10 is to "let them serve," which allows deacons to serve in any capacity as established by their elders. The initial issue that arose in the Jerusalem church was managed by apostle-appointed servants who would care for the widows. Scripture does not tell us if there were any issues or apostle-appointed servants after that one. Paul expanded the framework initiated in Acts 6 for local elders to appoint any needed tasks to deacons. Proper church leadership has deacons working in areas of service overseen by the elders on behalf of Christ for the body to the glory of God. Elders appoint these areas of service to assist, encourage, and help the body.

In our church, deacons serve and help manage facilities, prepare for service, open and close the campus on Sunday, manage ushers and greeters, manage campus security, help with technology, manage online resources and communications, manage communion preparation and clean up, baptism preparation and clean up, and more. Oddly enough, our elders manage the church benevolence and ministry to widows. This is our elders' preference.

---

[24] "By designating the officials of 1 Tim 3:8-13 as assistants and not table servers, Paul allows them to do other demanding tasks that would assist the elders in the "care for God's church" (1 Tim 3:5). The help of qualified, approved assistants who have the authority to carry out tasks delegated by the pastor elders relieves the elders of certain demanding tasks and helps them to keep their focus on their primary ministry of leading and feeding God's flock. The designation of such assistants is in keeping with the intent of the table-serving Seven appointed in the church in Jerusalem." Strauch, *Paul's Vision*, 74.

Length of Office Term

Scripture is silent about the term of office for elder and deacon. Many believe because of silence combined with the godly call to leadership that the position is for life.[25] Others desire to involve more men in leadership by creating a rotation of leaders with office terms. These believe office terms help to avoid overworking deacons and helps to remove ineffective deacons.[26]

Best practice

When Scripture is silent on an issue, it is common for many to turn to man's wisdom and create structures/systems to fill the void. If Christ, the head of the church, did not directly establish parameters in Scripture for addressing how long a deacon or elder is to serve, then what is to be done? Simply put, this falls under the authority of local church elders. If Christ does not speak to it, then he plans to work through the Spirit, guiding his under-shepherds, just as he does on many other issues.

In our church there are no established terms for elders or deacons. Deacons are accountable to the elders and we would not use terms to passively remove a bad deacon. We address those situations directly. There are three elements for a deacon's term of service:

1. He can serve as long as he is qualified.
2. He can serve as long as he desires the office.
3. He can serve as long as there are ministry needs in the church that require deacons.

Deacons have the ability to take a leave of absence if the issues of life require their church service to be set aside for a time to

---

[25] Gene A. Getz, *Elders and Leaders* (Chicago, IL: Moody Publishers, 2016), 305.
[26] Naylor, *The Baptist Deacon*, 50-54

properly attend to other responsibilities. Lastly, deacons can always remove themselves from office when they feel God is leading them to do so.

The potential of being overworked and removing bad leaders are the two primary reasons for terms. We trust that God will make known the need for more men in leadership and will add them accordingly. We keep all leaders accountable to each other to address issues of performance or qualifications, and we provide leaves of absence to help with heavy loads in life.

Other Bad Practices
Ordaining women deacons

As discussed in chapter eight, Scripture does not support women holding the formal office of deacon. Below are the major points highlighted from chapter eight:

1. The women in 1 Timothy 3:11 are the wives of deacons based on both the contextual and grammatical considerations of the entire passage.
2. All other New Testament references to women as deacons use the Greek word *diakonia* which is not the noun used by Paul to establish the office of deacon. These references lack the contextual and grammatical structures to support women deacons.
3. The one exception to point two is Phoebe in Romans 16:1. Paul uses the root of the *diakonos* noun, the same noun he used to formalize the office of deacons in 1 Timothy 3:8, 12 and Paul's formal address to church leaders Philippians 1:1. However, the noun is in the feminine accusative case and therefore does not match the

grammatical structure of 1 Timothy 3:8, 12 and Philippians 1:1. Some believe Romans 16:1 is contextually connected to the formal office of deacon, however, it does not match the grammatical structure and context given by Paul. This is why the Greek to English translation of Romans 16:1 has such diversity across the various English translations; "deacon," "deaconess," and "servant."

4. If Romans 16:1 is the scriptural foundation for women deacons, there is a void in Scripture that provides the role, qualifications of the office and how women deacons fit in the leadership structure. Since delegated authority from the elders is a major part of the deacon office, and Paul expressly stated that women are not to have authority over men (1 Tim 2:12), it stands to reason that Paul would have provided instructions on these issues.

5. The book of Romans was written in 55-57 AD, eight to ten years before Paul universalized the office in 1 Timothy 3.

In addition to the above, chapter five demonstrated the seriousness of the laying on of hands. This was a practice not often recorded in the New Testament. It displayed the unity of the church, its leaders, and members in setting apart men for a task. It was always performed on men either being ordained into leadership or sent to plant new churches.

For these reasons, ordaining women as deacons goes against Scripture. They are not to hold the formal office, and it is not in keeping with the practice of laying on hands.

Appendix 1: Best Practices

This does not keep elders of a local church from identifying women and giving them the title of deacon or deaconess. As we have discussed elders can delegate authority in the oversight of their church. However, doing so causes problems:

1. If elders choose to have women deacons/deaconesses, their purpose and role in the church needs to be clearly defined and explained to the body so they won't be mistaken as being part of the formal church leadership. It needs to be understood that they do not carry the delegated authority of the elders as a deacon does and they should not have authority over a man. They can manage tasks and coordinate ministries, but clear parameters need to be understood.

2. There are usually many servant positions headed by women in a church like the nursery, women's ministries, hospitality, the kitchen, meals, etc. Will these women be called women deacons/deaconesses? If so, the difference between other servant positions and women deacons/deaconesses needs to be properly understood and explained.

With titles come an understood purpose, role, authority and responsibility of a position. The elders need to be clear in their communication across all positions of the church. Blurry lines and unclear direction give way to confusion, ineffective operations, and hurt feelings. Wisdom and clarity are needed when establishing and managing church leadership and management structure.

Other Best Practices
Training and accountability
Elders and deacons should have a routine to continue training and ways to keep each other accountable. Building the bonds between elders and deacons are important for maintaining quality relationships, encouraging perseverance during difficult situations, modeling for the body. The leadership team needs to be praying for each other, sharing their lives, and being there for one another during difficult times. A routine of prayer for one another is basic. Special time set aside to meet is needed as well. Regular retreats once or twice a year are good get-a-ways for bonding, training, and coordination of duties.

Satan attacks leaders by trying to create division and unrest. Ecclesiastes 4:9-12 says we should labor together to help overcome oppressive forces:

> Two are better than one because they have a good return for their labor; for if either of them falls, the one will lift up his companion. But woe to the one who falls when there is not another to lift him up! Furthermore, if two lie down together they keep warm, but how can one be warm alone? And if one can overpower him who is *alone*, two can resist him. A cord of three *strands* is not quickly torn apart.

And let us not forget the wisdom of Solomon:

> As iron sharpens iron,
> So one person sharpens another (Prov 27:17, NASB).

Teaching and valuing leadership
The Apostle Paul taught and valued church leadership. One of

his five "trustworthy sayings" was on church leadership. These sayings were used in the early church to help God's people to remember his Word. As a church planter, Paul understood the importance of the proper structure and operations. He taught it to the leaders and the local congregations.

Judges 2:8-12 is a great reminder that if leadership does not constantly teach their people what they should value, the people, at best, will drift into spiritual mediocrity. When this happens in the church, Satan will use it to pull us away from the Lord. After Joshua's death, the next generation of Israelites were not taught the works of God and so they drifted away from God, eventually worshipping false gods.

Christ requires us to handle his Word with precision and accuracy. Sadly, within a few generations of the apostolic era, the church moved away from proper biblical leadership structures. We need to remember, follow, and teach the leadership structure Christ created for his church. Today, we have numerous church leadership structures, roles, practices, and traditions that do not match what Christ prescribed for his churches. Surely this pattern does not please the Lord who has given us a clear word on these matters.

Laying on of hands
The laying on of hands is used in the Bible to show the anointing of or moving of God's hand through his servants. In the Old Testament, priests laid hands on the animal sacrifices that were atoning for the sins of the people (2 Chron 29:20-24). Jesus laid his hands on people he healed (Mark 8:23; Luke 4:40). The church leaders of Antioch laid hands on Paul and Barnabas when sending them on the first missionary journey (Acts 13:3).

The most common use of laying hands was in the

ordination of leadership. In the Old Testament, laying of hands was a part of the anointing and ordination of priests (Num 3:1-3). Moses laid hands on Joshua, ordaining him as a leader of the people (Deut 34:9; Num 27:22-23). Throughout the New Testament, hands were laid on church leadership. Ananias laid hands on Paul after his conversion (Acts 9:17). The Ephesian elders laid hands on Timothy (1 Tim 4:14) and the apostles laid hands on the seven servants in Acts 6:6. The laying on of hands when installing new leaders is not commanded in Scripture, but it is a good practice that provides opportunity to teach the body by emphasizing the importance of the role a man is assuming on behalf of the church.

In our church, the crescendo of the selection process ends in a public ordination service. Our pastor-teacher will teach on the leadership role, review the selection process and the qualifications of the man, and provide an overview of the position being filled. The elders then surround the newly selected man, each praying about a specific topic: his new position, his family, his marriage, his service (past, present and future), God's protection, and more.

The public ordination service is one of the best tools to reinforce the teaching and modeling of Christ's leadership structure.

Job Descriptions
Written expectations bring clarity, are good for review/training, and provide documentation for reference if there is confusion in the future. Our church uses the job descriptions below as the foundation for church leadership.

Elders
Position Summary
Jesus is the Chief Shepherd of the universal and local church

Appendix 1: Best Practices

(1 Pet 5:4). Elders are Christ's under-shepherds of the local church and charged to be its leaders. Elders are to shepherd the flock that Christ has given them (1 Pet 5:2), feeding, guiding, protecting and caring for church members just as shepherds do with sheep.

Elders are subject to the Bible. "Above reproach" (1 Tim 3 and Titus 1), they are called to teach, lead and be models for their church body. Elders' efforts are in pursuit of a genuine, authentic relationship with Jesus Christ by applying their own God-transformed life to impact the lives of others.

The four primary duties of an elder:

- Teach Faithfully God's Word (Titus 1:9). An elder must be able teach (1 Tim 3:2) and have the ability to refute those who contradict it (Titus 1:9). He is responsible to oversee what's being taught throughout the venues of the church.

- Pray Devotedly for the Flock (Acts 6:4). Only through the power of the Holy Spirit and the Word of God can believers come to maturity in Christ. Prayer is a primary tool of an elder when properly shepherding God's flock.

- Lead Courageously (Acts 20:28, Eph 4:12-13). Leading believers to maturity in Christ requires elders to be proactive, strategic, and sometime confrontational to build up the Body.

- Model Inspiringly (1 Pet 5:3, 1 Cor 11:1, 1 Tim 3:1-7, Titus 1:5-16). The character qualities of an elder are essential and foundational if they are to be imitated by the flock. These include spiritually maturity, humility, transparency, approachability.

Essential Duties and Responsibilities
Spiritual Oversight

- Overseeing the theological foundations of the church

- Overseeing and implementing all elements of preaching, teaching, discipleship, counseling and ministry of the Word

- Overseeing all elements of worship including ordinances of baptism and the communion

- Overseeing and directing church discipline

- Overseeing ministry care of weddings, memorial services, visitation, etc.

Operational Oversight

- Overseeing all operations of the church

- Overseeing all financial and budget planning, capital and asset management

- Developing and initiating policy

Deacons

Position Summary
The church has a simple leadership structure: elders, who are the spiritual leaders, and deacons, who are servant leaders (1 Tim 3:1-13). Deacons primarily manage the physical and

logistical needs of the church at the direction of the elders (Acts 6:1-6).

Essential Duties and Responsibilities

- Facilities – managing critical areas of the church property; facility set-up and tear-down, fellowship meal preparations and clean up, communion preparations and clean up, and other events.

- Ministry Logistics – managing media, audio/visual, security, ushers/greeter, and other logistical areas.

- Character Model – Deacons are church leaders; as such, their character qualities are to be models for others to witness and desire to follow (1 Tim 3:8-12).

Appendix 2
Raising Deacons

Whether you are a church plant that has grown and now in need of deacons, or an established church that has not properly formalized the office of deacon, this appendix provides a step-by-step biblical process to raise-up deacons. There is no one universal method to find and establish deacons. Paul provided a high-level process in 1 Timothy 3:10 that was discussed in chapter five.

1. "Test" – a comprehensive examination of a deacon candidate by the body and elders
2. "Found blameless" – a determination the candidate meets all biblical requirements
3. "Let them serve" – lay hands and ordain them as deacon

Paul's process in v. 10 provides a general procedure and gives elders tremendous autonomy in fine-tuning the process for the local church. Paul's process starts with examination of a deacon candidate leaving to the local church elders the *assessment* and *identification* of deacon candidates. Our church elders use the process below.

Assessing the Need for Deacons

The model of Acts 6 is clear. Once tasks become burdensome for the elders and it is taking them away from the ministry of the word and prayer, deacons are needed. It is common for a deacon candidate to already be working in the ministry where help is needed. This has happened many times over the years at our church. In our young professional's ministry the abundance of events and coordination required a deacon. The candidate was already working in that ministry. I remember early in the discussions with him about becoming a deacon he asked, "What do you want me to do? I am already very busy with the young professional's ministry, do you want me to do other things too?" He was excited to know we wanted him to continue in the young professional's ministry leadership as a deacon to help the pastor in that ministry.

When do elders choose to have a deacon over a ministry area verses another member as a ministry leader? This is a good question and one without a direct answer. Ultimately it comes down to a decision of the elders and what they deem is best for the church. In Acts 6 the apostles' primary focus was on spiritual qualifications. Leaders that as they perform and implement tasks do it through a comprehensive spirit-filled lens. If that is the type of leader needed for the task the elders require, then a deacon is the answer. It is not always that easy which is why elders should approach the decision with pray and wisdom.

Identifying a Candidate

At least once a year our elders have a purposed discussion about future potential deacons. We bring up names of men that are solid servants and demonstrate the character qualities of 1 Timothy 3:8-12. We discuss our thoughts and experiences about each man to get every elder's input. We have this discussion even when there is not a pressing need for another deacon for the purpose of elder consensus around potential future leaders. Below are the items we discuss:

A. Current and past service – Deacons are to have the gift of serving. We discuss the depth and breadth of their service to make an initial assessment if they have the gift of serving.

B. Ownership in service – There are servants who simply do what is requested and the elders are always grateful for that service. Then there are those who go the extra mile in their service to bring a higher quality, improved excellence, take initiative, or help in coordination. These things also help to see the gift of service and potential of working with elders and other church servants.

C. Known by the body – Deacons need to be known by the body. As was seen in the selection process in both Acts 6: 3 and 1 Timothy 3:10 the members need to know the candidates to fully examine them.

D. Meets all qualifications – Deacons are church leaders and models to the membership. In the elders' initial discussions, many times we don't know the fullness of how the man measures across all character qualities listed in 1 Timothy 3:8-12. We affirm what we believe we already know and highlight the areas to know deeper about the potential deacon candidate. This includes how his wife measures in her qualifications in v. 11.

Our elders purposely have the annual conversation about deacons so that when it is time to bring on a deacon(s) for needed tasks there is a short list of men to consider. Additionally, it is helpful for all elders to know all the potential candidates for continued prayer and observation.

Discovery
When the elders have identified a need and chosen a potential deacon candidate an elder(s) will have a discovery meeting with the potential deacon candidate. Our church chooses to have one to two elders work with the deacon candidate through the process. That elder will provide regular progress updates to all the elders. We use the term "potential deacon candidate" until the man agrees to be considered and is ready to start the examination process. Then he becomes a formal deacon candidate.

At the initial meeting the elder(s) reveals the idea of deaconship and observes the initial reaction of the potential candidate. It is important to note that it is common for servants to have never considered being a servant-leader. It is common for men to be apprehensive and not think of themselves as formal church leaders. It is common to end the first meeting with the potential candidate thinking, praying and seeking God's wisdom about the position for one to two weeks.

Once a potential candidate has determined he is ready to be considered, the man becomes a formal deacon candidate. In our church the small circle of people that know about this are the elders, the deacon candidate, and his wife (if he is married). Then the next step of examination begins. It is not uncommon after a couple of weeks of prayer and seeking God's wisdom that the potential candidate does not feel led to the position. We make sure their apprehensiveness is not clouded in vague reasoning but is clear and specific understanding the call to leadership should not come from persuasion or coercion either. And of course, in these cases that potential candidacy is ended.

Elder Examination

After the discovery meeting(s) and the deacon candidate is ready to move forward. The elders are informed and regularly pray for God's will to be revealed in the examination process. In our church the process starts with an elder(s) having a series of meetings with the candidate to discuss each of the qualifications listed in 1 Timothy 3:8-12. Additional reading material on deacons may also be provided and discussed as the candidate is being fully vetted. One of the first qualifications to be discussed is proper aspiration to the office of deacon. As was discussed in chapter five, proper aspiration is a heart issue that is not easily discerned. A man with improper aspirations can cause tremendous damage to a church. Vetting the reasons a man feels led to the position is essential and should be equally scrutinized as all other nine qualifications. We will have several meetings to discuss these qualifications with two or three-weeks between meetings. Each meeting starts by reviewing the previous meeting. It is common for the elder and/or candidate to have questions about the previous meeting's discussion. This process should not be rushed. Take the time needed to walk through all the qualifications. This process will usually take a few months to complete. During this time the elders are regularly informed of the progress by the elder(s) working with the candidate.

If it is discovered the candidate is disqualified by one or more of the ten qualifications. The examination process is ended. The circle of people who know is still small--the elders, the candidate. and his wife. Depending on the nature of the disqualification the man may be considered again in the future.

After reviewing the ten qualifications with the candidate the elder(s) then has a meeting with the candidate and his wife. The purpose of the meeting is to get her input about the qualifications for her husband; review the qualifications of the deacon's wife in 1 Timothy 3:11; answer questions of what is expected of him and her if he becomes a deacon; prepare both husband and wife for the rest of the selection process; and encourage them with the promise of Christ in 1 Timothy 3:13.

A wife uniquely knows her husband, her input on how her husband measures across the ten deacon qualifications is important information for the elders. This is also the time to discuss how the wife sees herself measuring up to the qualifications of v. 11. The purpose is for the elders to know how each spouse thinks about the other on these biblical qualifications.

At our church when the elder(s) who have been working with the deacon candidate is satisfied (they meet all the qualifications) the next step is for the candidate to meet with several other deacons. The circle of people who know of the deacon candidacy now includes the elders and deacons. The two-fold purpose is first for the deacons to evaluate the candidate giving their feedback to the elders, and second, for the candidate to connect with deacons and talk freely about being a deacon.

If any concerns arise from the deacons' meeting with the candidate, the elder(s) who has been working with the candidate vets out the issue. If some disqualifying issue surfaces again the circle of people is small to help protect the reputation of the candidate and harmony with the church body is preserved. Once the deacons and elder(s) (who has been working with the candidate) are satisfied and the candidate meets all qualifications, it is time for the elders' interview(s).

The elders have been informed along each step of the process and given key insights. It is now time for the full group of elders to interview the candidate. Our churches preference is for a single meeting with all elders present. This way all elders get to hear the questions and answers at a single time limiting the chance of misunderstanding that can come from multiple smaller group meetings. Because of time constraints there may be a need for multiple meetings with the candidate, but all elders should be at all the meetings.

Once the elders have interviewed and confirmed the candidate is qualified to be a deacon, it is time to put him forward to the church body.

Church Member Examination

Up until the point the circle of people who knew about the deacon candidacy has been small: the elders, the deacons, the candidate, and his wife. If a disqualification arose in the discovery or elder examination phases the reputation of the candidate would be protected from the whole church knowing. A disqualification does not necessarily mean the man is leading a sinful life. It is common during the discovery phase the candidate for the first time fully grasps the leadership role expected of a deacon and after praying is led to not move forward. There are times during the elder examination the candidate sees he really does not aspire to leadership and decides to not move forward. There are times when there is a season of tough marriage or family issues and until those are resolve the candidate should not move forward. These reasons and others are why it is important to keep the circle people knowing about the candidacy small until it is time to take it to the body.

At this point the elders have thoroughly vetted the deacon candidate and are convinced, short of any unknown factor, he is ready to become a deacon.

1. The elders were potentially watching him for monthly or years prior to them approaching him to become a candidate.

2. The elders have thoroughly examined his qualifications including input from his wife and current deacons and deemed worthy to put forward to the body.

3. The candidate has examined his heart and believes this is God's will and is ready to be put forward to the body.

Now it is time to involve the church body. At our church this starts with a letter/email from the elders to all members. The email provides the candidates background, past and current service, and general details of the elders' examination of the candidate over a number of months. The letter acknowledges the elders' enthusiasm for the candidate and requests essentially needed input from the members. We ask the members to contact a designated elder with any endorsement or concern about the candidate within a three-week window. Endorsements for forwarded to the candidate and all elders. Concerns are vetted out by the designated elder.

Appendix 2: Raising Deacons

Concerns need to be validated and investigated. Unlike the congregational approach of voting on a candidate where the majority rules. Here a single concern from a single person could disqualify a candidate. Often, during the member examination an unresolved issue between a candidate and another party comes out. This is a good thing. Unresolved issues between brothers and sisters in Christ is not good. It creates resentment, harbors ill will, and brings disharmony to the body. Especially if it involves leaders. This affords the opportunity to get things right. If this is an issue of offence or preference the one with the concern and the candidate will meet to resolve the issue. Once resolved the designated elder will confirm with the person who was concerned, if they are okay moving forward with the candidate. He will then let the elders know there was a conflict, the nature of the conflict and that is has been resolved. If the concern is an unrepentant sin then step-one of Matthew 18:15-20 between the candidate and person concerned is taken. Depending how the issue is or is not resolved could disqualify the candidate. If the concern is around character qualities of 1 Timothy 3 or other Scripture i.e., the candidate at his employment acts and lives differently that is not consistent with proper Christian character. This needs to be investigated and may result in the Matthew 18 process as well. Any legitimate concern from the body requires elders to pray and seek God's will.

After the member examination phase if there are no unaddressed or outstanding concerns the elders have one final meeting to confirm all feedback and move to ordain the candidate. Once an ordination date is set the results of the member examination and ordination date is communicated to the body.

After the member examination, if there are any unresolved issues the elder need to decide what should be communicated to the body. If there is a disqualification during the member examination care needs taken in the communication especially if there is no sin issue.

Ordination

At our church ordination is done at a Sunday service. Our pastor-teacher will start with a brief overview, giving the background of the new deacon and the process of elder and member examination. He will have the deacon and his wife come up to the front and have the elders surround the deacon lay hands on him and pray for him. Each elder will prays for a specific topic; continued faithful service; their marriage and family; spiritual protection; integrity and character; relationship with God; etc.

Bibliography

A. Duane Litfin, *The Bible Knowledge Commentary: New Testament Edition*, ed. John F. Walvoord and Roy B. Zuck (Wheaton, IL: Victor Books, 1986).

A. T. Robertson, *Word Picture in the New Testament, Vol. III* (Grand Rapids, MI: Baker Book House, 1930).

Adam Clarke, *Clarke's Commentary, Vol. VI: Romans to Revelation* (New York: Abingdon Press, 1900).

Albert Mohler, *The Conviction to Lead* (Minneapolis, MN: Bethany House Publishers, 2012).

Alexander Strauch, *The New Testament Deacon* (Littleton, CO: Lewis & Roth Publishers, 1992).

Alexander Strauch, *Paul's Vision for the Deacons* (Littleton, CO: Lewis and Roth Publishers, 2017).

Benjamin Merkle, *40 Questions About Elders and Deacons* (Grand Rapids, MI: Kregel Publications, 2008).

Benjamin Merkle, "The Authority of Deacons in Pauline Churches," *Journal of the Evangelical Theological Society, Vol. 64* (Scottsdale, AZ, 2021).

"Catholic Priests – Hierarchy, Roles, and Requirements," Scripture Catholic, last modified 2022, https://www.scripturecatholic.com/catholic-priests/.

Christina Hip-Flores, "Consecrated Widows: A Restored Ancient Vocation in the Catholic Church," *Logos: A Journal of Catholic Thought and Culture 22, no. 1* (Winter 2019).

Cliff McManis, *The Biblically-Driven Church* (Cupertino, CA: With All Wisdom Publications, 2016).

Cornelis Van Dam, *The Deacon: Biblical Foundations for Today's Ministry of Mercy* (Grand Rapids, MI: Reformation Heritage Books, 2016).

David G. Peterson, "First Timothy," *The Pillar New Testament Commentary*, ed. D.A. Carson (Grand Rapids, MI: Eerdmans, 2009).

"Deacon Ministry," Church of the Brethren, last modified 2022, https://www.brethren.org/discipleshipmin/deacons/.

"Deacons and Diaconal Ministers," Resource UMC, last modified 2018, https://www.resourceumc.org/en/content/deacons-and-diaconal-ministers.

Donald Guthrie, *Tyndale New Testament Commentaries: The Pastoral Epistles* (Grand Rapids, MI: Eerdmans Publishing Company, 1980).

Earl S. Johnson, Jr., "The Presbyterian Deacon," *The Presbyterian Outlook*, August 31, 2008.

Everett Harrison, *The Expositor's Bible Commentary: Romans, Vol. 10* (Grand Rapids, MI: Zondervan, 1976).

Francis Martin and Thomas Oden, *Acts: Ancient Christian Commentary on Scripture – New Testament, Vol. 5* (Downers

Grove, IL: InterVaristy Press, 2006).

Gene A. Getz, *Elders and Leaders* (Chicago, IL: Moody Publishers, 2016).

Gerhard Kittle, ed., *Theological Dictionary of the New Testament, Vol. II* (Grand Rapids, MI: Eerdmans Publishing Co., 1964).

Gordon D. Fee, *New International Biblical Commentary: 1 and 2 Timothy, Titus* (Peabody, MA: Hendrickson Publishers, 1988).

Gregg R. Allison, *Sojourners and Strangers: The Doctrine of the Church* (Wheaton, IL: Crossway, 2012).

H.C.G. Moule, *Studies in Philippians* (Grand Rapids, MI: Kregel Publications, 1977).

Harold Nichols, *The Work of the Deacon & Deaconess* (Valley Forge, PA: Judson Press, 2014).

Henry W. Holloman, *Kregel Dictionary of the Bible and Theology* (Grand Rapids, MI: Kregel Publications, 2005).

Henry Webb, *Deacons: Servant Models in the Church* (Nashville, TN: B&H Publishing Group, 2001).

Homer A. Kent, Jr., *The Pastoral Epistles* (Winona Lake, IN: BMH Books, 1995).

Howard B. Foshee, *Now That You're a Deacon* (Nashville, TN: B&H Publishing Group, 1975).

Howard Sugden and Warren Wiersbe, *Confident Pastoral Leadership* (Chicago, IL: Moody Press, 1973).

I.H. Marshall and Philip H. Towner, *The Pastoral Epistles* (London: T&T Clark, 2004).

J.D. O'Donnell, *Handbook for Deacons* (Nashville, TN: Randall House Publications, 1973).

James Moulton and George Milligan, *The Vocabulary of the Greek New Testament* (Grand Rapids, MI: Eerdmans Publishing, 1930).

Jeannine Olson, *Deacon and Deaconesses Through the Centuries* (St. Louis, MO: Concordia Publishing House, 2005).

John Calvin, *Commentaries on the Epistles to Timothy, Titus, and Philemon, Vol. XXI*, translated by William Pringle (Grand Rapids, MI: Baker Book House, 2003).

John Calvin, *Institutes of the Christian Religion*, translated by Henry Beveridge (Peabody, MA: Hendrickson Publishers, 2008).

John Koessler, "1 Timothy," *The Moody Bible Commentary*, ed. Michael Rydelink and Michael Vanlaningham (Chicago, IL: Moody Publishers, 2014).

John M. Frame, *Systematic Theology: An Introduction to Christian Belief* (Phillipsburg, NJ: P&R Publishing, 2013).

John MacArthur, *The MacArthur New Testament Commentary: Acts* (Chicago, IL: The Moody Bible Institute, 1994).

John MacArthur, *The MacArthur New Testament Commentary: 1 Timothy* (Chicago, IL: Moody Publishers, 1995).

John MacArthur and Richard Mayhue, *Biblical Doctrine: A Systematic Summary of Bible Truth* (Wheaton, IL: Crossway, 2017).

Bibliography

Malcolm O. Tolbert, *Layman's Bible Book Commentary – Colossians, Philippians, 1 & 2 Thessalonians, 1 & 2 Timothy, Titus, Philemon, Vol. 22* (Nashville, TN: Broadman Press, 1980).

Matthew Henry, *Matthew Henry's Commentary on the Whole Bible – Vol. VI Acts to Revelation* (McLean, VA: MacDonald Publishing Company, 1980).

Merrill F. Unger, *The New Unger's Bible Dictionary* (Chicago, IL: Moody Publishers, 2006).

Millard J. Erickson, *Christian Theology, 2nd ed.* (Grand Rapids, MI, Baker, 1988).

Norman L. Geisler, *A Popular Survey of the New Testament* (Ada, MI: Baker Books, 2007).

R. C. H. Lenski, *The Interpretation of The Acts of the Apostles* (Columbus, OH: The Wartburg Press, 1944).

Ralph Earle, *The Expositor's Bible Commentary: 1, 2 Timothy, Vol. 11*, ed., Frank E. Gaebelein (Grand Rapids, MI: Zondervan Publishing House, 1976).

Rick Warren, *The Purpose Driven Church* (Grand Rapids, MI: The Zondervan Corporation, 1995).

Richard N. Longenecker, *The Expositor's Bible Commentary – Vol. 9* (Grand Rapids, MI: The Zondervan Corporation. 1984).

Robert H. Gundry, *Commentary on the New Testament* (Peabody, MA: Hendrickson Publishers, 2010).

Robert Maddox, Jr., *Layman's Bible Book Commentary – Acts, Vol. 19* (Nashville, TN: Broadman Press, 1979).

Robert Naylor, *The Baptist Deacon* (Nashville, TN: Broadman and Holman Publishers, 1955).

Robert P. Lightner, *The Bible Knowledge Commentary: Philippians*, ed. John F. Walvoord and Roy B. Zuck (Wheaton, IL: Victor Books, 1986).

Sr Bernadette Mary Rei, "Pope Institutes New Commission to Study Women Deacons," *Vatican News*, April 8, 2020, https://www.vaticannews.va/en/pope/news/2020-04/pope-commission-women-deacons.html.

Stanley D. Toussaint, *The Bible Knowledge Commentary – New Testament* (USA: Victor Books, 1983).

Thabiti M. Anyabwile, *Finding Faithful Elders and Deacons* (Wheaton, IL: Crossway, 2012).

"The Ministry of a Deacon and Provisional Deacon," BOM Library, last modified January 2013, https://www.bomlibrary.org/wp-content/uploads/2015/06/Guide-for-Deacons.pdf.

The NET Bible: New English Translation (Thomas Nelson, 2019).

Thomas R. Schreiner, *Romans* (Grand Rapids, MI: Baker Academic, 2018).

Walter Bauer, *A Greek-English Lexicon of the New Testament and Other Early Christian Literature* (Chicago, IL: University of Chicago Press, 2001).

William Hendriksen, *New Testament Commentary: Thessalonians, Timothy and Titus* (Grand Rapids, MI: Baker Book House, 1990).

Scripture Index

Genesis
1:28...............51
2:18-24..........87
2:20-24..........51
3:1-6............141

Exodus
18:17-26.....146

Numbers
3:1-3............176
11:16...........150
27:22-23.....176

Deuteronomy
6:4-7.............89
17:14-17.......51
34:9.............176

Judges
2:8-11...........90
2:8-12.........175
2:10.............106

1 Samuel
10:1..............51

1 Kings
2:3-4.............51

2 Chronicles
29:20-24.....175

Proverbs
20:1..............82
27:17...........174

Ecclesiastes
4:9-12..........174

Isaiah
9:16..............12
40:6-31.........10

Matthew
4:1-11...11, 141
5:18..............11
5:23-24........104
5:28............118

Matthew
5:32............118
7:21-23...........9
12:1-8...........11
16:18..............7, 8, 9, 140
18:15-17.....164
18:15-20....103, 189
19:3-9...........88
22:13.............29
25:21.............85
27:11.............44
28:18..............9

Mark
1:13..............30
1:31..............30
8:23............175
10:45.............30
15:40-41.....125

Luke
2:36-38.......125

Luke
4:39.............30
4:40............175
8:2-3...........125
10:38...........125
10:39...........125
10:40............30
12:37............30
17:8.............30
20:46-47.........82
22:9.............82
22:26............30
22:27............30
22:31...........113
24:10...........124, 125

John
1:1-5............10
2:9..............81
10:27-30.........10
12:2.............30
12:26............30
13:34-35.........34, 126
14:2-3...........10
21:15-17........144, 159
21:17............9, 11

Acts
1:14............125
1:17.............30
1:25.............30
2:1-47............9
2:41............39, 58
2:42............100
2:47.............39
4:4............39, 107
4:32-35.........100
4:34-35..........55
4:35.............23
5:14.............39
6:1..............30
6:1-3...........144
6:1-6...........31, 35, 58, 179
6:1-7...........36, 39
6:2............30, 38, 51, 144
6:2-4, 6........145
6:3............51, 53, 76, 81, 156
6:4............30, 177
6:5.............75, 77
6:6............42, 43, 54, 100, 164, 176
6:7............58, 92, 101, 107, 111, 142, 144, 146
6:8-11...........90
9:17............176
9:36-42.........125
11:29............30

Acts
12:12...........125
12:13-15........125
12:25............30
13:1-3...........54
13:3............175
14:23...........102, 143, 150
15:36-40........161
16:40...........125
17:11...........147
18:18...........125
19:22............30
20:24............30
20:28............55, 99, 177
21:9............125
21:19............30
28:14-31.........32

Romans
8:34..............9
11:13............30
12:6-8..........101
12:7............2, 30, 77
13:4.............29
15:8...........29, 136
15:25............30
16:1............32, 33, 114, 123, 125, 133, 134, 135, 136, 137, 138, 171, 172
16:1-15........31, 32

Romans
16:6............125
16:7............125
16:12...........125
16:13...........125
16:15...........125

1 Corinthians
1:11............125
4:6.............157
7:1-5............88
7:2............119
10:31...........111
11:8-9..........119
12:3............101
12:5.............30
12:11...........102
12:28........77, 91
14:34...........119
14:40............10
15:1-4............9
16:15............30

2 Corinthians
1:12.............83
3:3..............30
3:6..............29
3:7..............30
3:8..............30
3:9..............30
8:19.............30
8:20.............30
11:15............29

Galatians
5:16-24..........82
5:22.............85
5:22-23..........53

Galatians
6:4..............79

Ephesians
3:7.........28, 136
3:14-19........106
4:11-12..........49
4:12.............30
5:15............148
5:18.............82
5:22-33..........88
5:23..........7, 8, 140, 141
5:23, 25..........9
5:24.............10
5:25-27..........10
5:26..............9
5:29..............9
6:4..............89
6:21.......28, 136

Philippians
1:1.........26, 28, 31, 32, 35, 134, 135, 171, 172
1:8-10..........147
4:2-3...........125

Colossians
1:7....26, 28, 33, 136
4:17.............30

1 Thess
5:23............161

1 Timothy
1:12.............30
1:15.............73
2:1-15..........122
2:8..............70
2:9-10........31, 33, 34, 35
2:9-15..........121
2:10............124
2:12...........126, 136, 172
2:12-14........131
2:14............119
3:1..............73
3:1-13....50, 70, 74, 77, 124, 126, 131, 138, 141, 142, 151, 178
3:1-7......3, 132, 177
3:2..........2, 101, 177
3:5.............169
3:6-7...........112
3:8..............28
3:8-10..........127
3:8-12........2, 3, 51, 104, 127, 154, 155, 156, 163, 179, 182, 183, 185

cxcix

1 Timothy
3:8-13............31, 35, 36, 39, 47, 48, 49, 55, 56, 58, 64, 69, 76, 143, 169
3:8-9, 12........53
3:8, 12.....28, 32, 35, 134, 135, 171, 172
3:10........30, 62, 63, 66, 74, 76, 78, 92, 93, 96, 100, 104, 105, 142, 144, 158, 159, 163, 167, 169, 181, 183
3:11........75, 93, 114, 115, 116, 118, 120, 138, 171, 186
3:12........28, 75
3:13........30, 75, 110, 111, 133, 186
3:15...............47
4:6.........28, 33, 136

1 Timothy
4:8-9...............73
4:11-16.......100
4:12...............21
4:14.......54, 176
5:9...............119
5:9-10...........33, 124
5:9-13....31, 34, 35
5:22, 24-25...79
5:23...............82
6:3-10............82
1:18...............30

2 Timothy
2:11...............73
2:12.............138
2:15.............137
3:14.............106
3:14-17.......137
4:2...............100
4:5.................30
4:11........30, 161
4:21.............125

Titus
1:5..........50, 54, 102, 143, 146, 150
1:5-9................3
1:6.................89
1:9......101, 102, 177

Titus
1:11...............82
3:8...............73

Philemon
1....................125
13.................31

Hebrews
1:14...............30
5:4.................15
6:10...............31
13:17.......11, 22

James
1:8.................81

1 Peter
1:12...............31
3:8.................88
4:10...............31
4:10-11.......102
4:11...............31
5:1...............100
5:1-2...........142
5:1-4.......22, 55
5:4............9, 10, 177
5:8.............113

Revelation
2:19...............30
22:18-19.......11

ABOUT THE AUTHOR

J. Robert Douglas is the executive pastor of Creekside Bible Church in Cupertino, California. He is a board member of The Cornerstone Bible College and Seminary, as well as several other Christian ministries. He lives with his wife, Robin, and their family in the San Francisco Bay Area.

About With All Wisdom

With All Wisdom is the Christian media creation ministry located in Cupertino, CA. We started this publishing ministry out of the simple desire to serve the local body with substantive biblical resources for the sake of our people's growth and spiritual maturity.

But we also believe that book publishing, like any other Christian ministry, should first and foremost be under the supervision and accountability of the local church. While we are grateful for and will continue to support the many excellent traditional publishers available today—our shelves are full of the books they have produced—we also believe that the best place to develop solid, life-giving theology and biblical instruction is within the local church.

With All Wisdom is also unique because we offer our books at a very low cost. We strive for excellence in our writing and seek to provide a high-quality product to our readers. Our editorial team is comprised of men and women who are highly trained and excellent in their craft. But since we are able to avoid the high overhead costs that are typically incurred by traditional publishers, we are able to pass significant savings on to you. The result is a growing collection of books that are substantive, readable, and affordable.

In order to best serve various spiritual and theological needs of the body of Christ, we have developed three distinct lines of books. **Big Truth | little books**® provides readers with accessible, manageable works on theology, Christian living, and important church and social issues in a format that is easy to read and easy to finish. Our **Equip Series** is aimed at Christians who desire to delve a little deeper into doctrine and practical matters of the faith. Our **Foundations Series** is our academic line in which we seek to contribute to the contemporary theological discussion by combining pastoral perspective with rigorous scholarship.

OTHER TITLES FROM WITH ALL WISDOM PUBLICATIONS

Please visit us at WithAllWisdom.org
to learn more about these titles

BIG TRUTH little books®
A Biblical View of Trials
Cliff McManis

What the Bible Says About Gray Areas
Cliff McManis

Faith: The Gift of God
Cliff McManis

The Problem of Evil
Cliff McManis

What the Bible Says About Government
Cliff McManis

God Defines and Defends Marriage
Cliff McManis

How to Pray for Your Pastor
Derek Brown

Protecting the Flock: The Priority of Church Membership
Cliff McManis

Educating Your Child: Public, Private, or Homeschool? A Biblical Perspective
Cliff McManis

What the Bible Says About Depression
Cliff McManis

What the Bible Says About Confrontation
Cliff McManis

Fellowship with God:
A Guide to Bible Reading, Meditation, and Prayer
Derek Brown

What the Bible Says About Hospitality
Cliff McManis

The Danger of Hypocrisy:
Coming to Grips with Jesus' Most Damning Sermon
J.R. Cuevas

Solomon's Great Commission: A Theology of Earthly Life
Derek Brown

What the Bible Says About the Future
Colin Eakin

The Parable of Sports
J.R. Cuevas

What the Bible Says About Retirement
Derek Brown and Cliff McManis

Equip
*The Biblically-Driven Church:
How Jesus Builds His Body*
Cliff McManis

*God's Glorious Story:
The Truth of What It's All About*
Colin Eakin

*Strong and Courageous:
The Character and Calling of Mature Manhood*
Derek Brown

*The Gospel, the Church, and Homosexuality:
How the Gospel is Still the Power of God
for Redemption and Transformation*
Edited by Michael Sanelli and Derek Brown

*Skillfully Surveying the Scriptures, Volume 1: Genesis
Through Esther*
J.R. Cuevas

Beware of Dogs: Exposing Error in the Modern Church
Colin Eakin

What the Bible Says About Israel: Past, Present & Future
Cliff McManis

Rescued by Grace, Volume 2: More Evidence that God is Still Saving Sinners
Edited by Cliff McManis and Derek Brown

Foundations
Apologetics by the Book
Cliff McManis

Made in the USA
Monee, IL
13 September 2023

42689409R00132